Let's Keep in Touch

Follow Us Online

Visit US at https://www.facebook.com/Effortlessmath

www.EffortlessMath.com https://goo.gl/2B6qWW

Online Math Lessons

It's easy! Here's how it works.

1- Request a FREE introductory session.
2- Meet a Math tutor online.
3- Start Learning Math in Minutes.

Send Email to: info@EffortlessMath.com

www.EffortlessMath.com

... So Much More Online!

- ✓ FREE Math lessons

- ✓ More Math learning books!

- ✓ Mathematics Worksheets

- ✓ Online Math Tutors

Need a PDF version of this book?

Send email to: info@EffortlessMath.com

FSA Mathematics Workbook For Grade 8

Step-By-Step Guide to Preparing for the FSA Math Test 2019

By

Reza Nazari

& Ava Ross

Copyright © 2018

Reza Nazari & Ava Ross

All rights reserved. No part of this publication may be reproduced, stored in a retrieval system, or transmitted in any form or by any means, electronic, mechanical, photocopying, recording, scanning, or otherwise, except as permitted under Section 107 or 108 of the 1976 United States Copyright Ac, without permission of the author.

All inquiries should be addressed to:

info@effortlessMath.com

www.EffortlessMath.com

ISBN-13: 978-1725822429

ISBN-10: 1725822423

Published by: Effortless Math Education

www.EffortlessMath.com

Description

The goal of this book is simple. It will help your student incorporates the best method and the right strategies to prepare for the FSA Mathematics test FAST and EFFECTIVELY.

FSA Mathematics Workbook is full of specific and detailed material that will be key to succeeding on the FSA Math. It's filled with the critical math concepts a student will need in order to ace the test. Math concepts in this book break down the topics, so the material can be quickly grasped. Examples are worked step-by-step, so you learn exactly what to do.

FSA Mathematics Workbook helps your student to focus on all Math topics that students will need to ace the FSA Math test. This book with 2 complete FSA tests is all your student will ever need to fully prepare for the FSA Math.

This workbook includes practice test questions. It contains easy-to-read essential summaries that highlight the key areas of the FSA Math test. Effortless Math test study guide reviews the most important components of the FSA Math test. Anyone planning to take the FSA Math test should take advantage of the review material and practice test questions contained in this study guide.

Inside the pages of this workbook, students can learn basic math operations in a structured manner with a complete study program to help them understand essential math skills. It also has many exciting features, including:

- Dynamic design and easy-to-follow activities
- A fun, interactive and concrete learning process
- Targeted, skill-building practices
- Math topics are grouped by category, so students can focus on the topics they struggle on
- All solutions for the exercises are included, so you will always find the answers
- 2 Complete FSA Math Practice Tests that reflect the format and question types on FSA

FSA Mathematics Workbook is a breakthrough in Math learning — offering a winning formula and the most powerful methods for learning basic Math topics confidently. Each section offers step-by-step instruction and helpful hints, with a few topics being tackled each chapter. Two complete REAL FSA Math tests are provided at the back of the book to refine your student's Math skills.

***FSA Mathematics Workbook* is the only book your student will ever need to master Basic Math topics!** It can be used as a self-study course - you do not need to work with a Math tutor. (It can also be used with a Math tutor).

Ideal for self-study as well as for classroom usage.

About the Author

Reza Nazari is the author of more than 100 Math learning books including:
– **Math and Critical Thinking Challenges:** For the Middle and High School Student
– **GED Math in 30 Days**
– **ASVAB Math Workbook 2018 - 2019**
– **Effortless Math Education Workbooks**
– and many more Mathematics books ...

Reza is also an experienced Math instructor and a test–prep expert who has been tutoring students since 2008. Reza is the founder of Effortless Math Education, a tutoring company that has helped many students raise their standardized test scores—and attend the colleges of their dreams. Reza provides an individualized custom learning plan and the personalized attention that makes a difference in how students view math.

You can contact Reza via email at:
reza@EffortlessMath.com

Find Reza's professional profile at:
goo.gl/zoC9rJ

Contents

Chapter 1: Fractions and Decimals 11
- Simplifying Fractions 12
- Adding and Subtracting Fractions 13
- Multiplying and Dividing Fractions 14
- Adding Mixed Numbers 15
- Subtract Mixed Numbers 16
- Multiplying Mixed Numbers 17
- Dividing Mixed Numbers 18
- Comparing Decimals 19
- Rounding Decimals 20
- Adding and Subtracting Decimals 21
- Multiplying and Dividing Decimals 22
- Converting Between Fractions, Decimals and Mixed Numbers 23
- Factoring Numbers 24
- Greatest Common Factor 25
- Least Common Multiple 26
- Test Preparation 27
- Answers of Worksheets – Chapter 1 29

Chapter 2: Real Numbers and Integers 36
- Adding and Subtracting Integers 37
- Multiplying and Dividing Integers 38
- Ordering Integers and Numbers 39
- Arrange, Order, and Comparing Integers 40
- Order of Operations 41
- Mixed Integer Computations 42
- Integers and Absolute Value 43
- Test Preparation 44
- Answers of Worksheets – Chapter 2 46

Chapter 3: Proportions and Ratios 50
- Writing Ratios 51
- Simplifying Ratios 52

Create a Proportion 53
Similar Figures 54
Simple Interest 55
Ratio and Rates Word Problems 56
Test Preparation 57
Answers of Worksheets – Chapter 3 60

Chapter 4: Percent 64
Percentage Calculations... 65
Converting Between Percent, Fractions, and Decimals... 66
Percent Problems 67
Find What Percentage a Number Is of Another 68
Find a Percentage of a Given Number 69
Percent of Increase and Decrease 70
Markup, Discount, and Tax 71
Test Preparation 72
Answers of Worksheets – Chapter 4 74

Chapter 5: Algebraic Expressions 79
Expressions and Variables.. 80
Simplifying Variable Expressions 81
Simplifying Polynomial Expressions... 82
Translate Phrases into an Algebraic Statement 83
The Distributive Property... 84
Evaluating One Variable... 85
Evaluating Two Variables 86
Combining like Terms 87
Test Preparation 88
Answers of Worksheets – Chapter 5 90

Chapter 6: Equations 94
One–Step Equations 95
One–Step Equation Word Problems.. 96
Two–Step Equations 97
Two–Step Equation Word Problems.. 98

Multi–Step Equations 99
Test Preparation 100
Answers of Worksheets – Chapter 6 102

Chapter 7: Systems of Equations 106
Solving Systems of Equations by Substitution 107
Solving Systems of Equations by Elimination 108
Systems of Equations Word Problems 109
Test Preparation 110
Answers of Worksheets – Chapter 7 111

Chapter 8: Inequalities 113
Graphing Single–Variable Inequalities 114
One–Step Inequalities 115
Two–Step Inequalities 116
Multi–Step Inequalities 117
Test Preparation 118
Answers of Worksheets – Chapter 8 121

Chapter 9: Linear Functions 125
Finding Slope 126
Graphing Lines Using Slope–Intercept Form 127
Graphing Lines Using Standard Form 128
Writing Linear Equations 129
Graphing Linear Inequalities 130
Finding Midpoint 131
Finding Distance of Two Points 132
Slope and Rate of Change 133
Find the Slope, x–intercept and y–intercept 134
Write an Equation from a Graph 135
Slope–intercept Form 136
Point–slope Form 137
Equations of Horizontal and Vertical Lines 138
Equation of Parallel or Perpendicular Lines 139
Test Preparation 140
Answers of Worksheets – Chapter 9 142

Chapter 10: Monomials and Polynomials 150
  Classifying Polynomials 151
  Writing Polynomials in Standard Form 152
  Simplifying Polynomials 153
  Add and Subtract monomials 154
  Multiplying Monomials 155
  Multiplying and Dividing Monomials 156
  GCF of Monomials 157
  Powers of monomials 158
  Multiplying a Polynomial and a Monomial 159
  Multiplying Binomials 160
  Factoring Trinomials 161
  Test Preparation 162
  Answers of Worksheets – Chapter 10 164

Chapter 11: Exponents and Radicals 170
  Multiplication Property of Exponents 171
  Division Property of Exponents 172
  Powers of Products and Quotients 173
  Zero and Negative Exponents 174
  Negative Exponents and Negative Bases 175
  Writing Scientific Notation 176
  Square Roots 177
  Test Preparation 178
  Answers of Worksheets – Chapter 11 180

Chapter 12: Plane Figures 184
  Transformations: Translations, Rotations, and Reflections 185
  The Pythagorean Theorem 186
  Area of Triangles 187
  Perimeter of Polygons 188
  Area and Circumference of Circles 189
  Area of Squares, Rectangles, and Parallelograms 190
  Area of Trapezoids 191

Test Preparation 192

Answers of Worksheets – Chapter 12 194

Test Preparation Answers 195

Chapter 13: Solid Figures 196

Volume of Cubes and Rectangle Prisms 197

Surface Area of Cubes 198

Surface Area of a Prism 199

Volume of Pyramids and Cones 200

Surface Area of Pyramids and Cones 201

Test Preparation 202

Answers of Worksheets – Chapter 13 203

Chapter 14: Statistics 205

Mean, Median, Mode, and Range of the Given Data 206

First Quartile, Second Quartile and Third Quartile of the Given Data 207

Box and Whisker Plots 208

Bar Graph 209

Stem–And–Leaf Plot 210

The Pie Graph or Circle Graph 211

Scatter Plots 212

Test Preparation 213

Answers of Worksheets – Chapter 14 215

Chapter 15: Probability 220

Probability of Simple Events 221

Experimental Probability 222

Factorials 223

Permutations 224

Combination 225

Test Preparation 226

Answers of Worksheets – Chapter 15 227

FSA Mathematics Practice Tests 230

FSA Mathematics Practice Test 1 231

FSA Mathematics Practice Test 2 258

FSA Practice Tests Answers and Explanations 284

Chapter 1: Fractions and Decimals

Topics that you'll learn in this chapter:

- ✓ Simplifying Fractions
- ✓ Adding and Subtracting Fractions
- ✓ Multiplying and Dividing Fractions
- ✓ Adding Mixed Numbers
- ✓ Subtract Mixed Numbers
- ✓ Multiplying Mixed Numbers
- ✓ Dividing Mixed Numbers
- ✓ Comparing Decimals
- ✓ Rounding Decimals
- ✓ Adding and Subtracting Decimals
- ✓ Multiplying and Dividing Decimals
- ✓ Converting Between Fractions, Decimals and Mixed Numbers
- ✓ Factoring Numbers
- ✓ Greatest Common Factor
- ✓ Least Common Multiple
- ✓ Divisibility Rules

Simplifying Fractions

Helpful Hints
- Evenly divide both the top and bottom of the fraction by 2, 3, 5, 7, ... etc.
- Continue until you can't go any further.

Example:
$$\frac{4}{12} = \frac{2}{6} = \frac{1}{3}$$

✏️ Simplify the fractions.

1) $\frac{22}{36} = \frac{11}{18}$ ✓

2) $\frac{8}{10} = \frac{4}{5}$ ✓

3) $\frac{12}{18} = \frac{4}{6} = \frac{2}{3}$ ✓

4) $\frac{6}{8} = \frac{3}{4}$ ✓

5) $\frac{13}{39} = \frac{13}{39}$ ✗

6) $\frac{5}{20} = \frac{1}{4}$ ✓

7) $\frac{16}{36} = \frac{1}{18}$ ✗

8) $\frac{18}{36} = \frac{2}{4} = \frac{1}{2}$ ✓

9) $\frac{20}{50} = \frac{2}{5}$ ✓

10) $\frac{6}{54} = \frac{1}{9}$ ✓

11) $\frac{45}{81} = \frac{5}{9}$ ✓

12) $\frac{21}{28} = \frac{3}{4}$ ✓

13) $\frac{35}{56} = \frac{5}{8}$ ✓

14) $\frac{52}{64} = \frac{13}{8}$ ✗

15) $\frac{13}{65} = \frac{13}{13} = 1$ ✗

16) $\frac{44}{77} = \frac{4}{7}$ ✓

17) $\frac{21}{42} = \frac{3}{6} = \frac{1}{2}$ ✓

18) $\frac{15}{36} = \frac{5}{12}$ ✓

19) $\frac{9}{24} = \frac{3}{8}$ ✓

20) $\frac{20}{80} = \frac{2}{8} = \frac{1}{4}$ ✓

21) $\frac{25}{45} = \frac{5}{9}$ ✓

FSA Mathematics Workbook For Grade 8

Adding and Subtracting Fractions

Helpful Hints
- For "like" fractions (fractions with the same denominator), add or subtract the numerators and write the answer over the common denominator.
- Find equivalent fractions with the same denominator before you can add or subtract fractions with different denominators.
- Adding and Subtracting with the same denominator:

$$\frac{a}{b} + \frac{c}{b} = \frac{a+c}{b}$$
$$\frac{a}{b} - \frac{c}{b} = \frac{a-c}{b}$$

- Adding and Subtracting fractions with different denominators:

$$\frac{a}{b} + \frac{c}{d} = \frac{ad+cb}{bd}$$
$$\frac{a}{b} - \frac{c}{d} = \frac{ad-cb}{bd}$$

1/18   F

✎ Add fractions.

✗ 1) $\frac{2}{3} + \frac{1}{2} = \frac{3}{6}$

✗ 4) $\frac{7}{4} + \frac{5}{9} = \frac{12}{36}$

✗ 7) $\frac{3}{4} + \frac{2}{5} = \frac{5}{20}$

✗ 2) $\frac{3}{5} + \frac{1}{3} = \frac{4}{15}$

✓ 5) $\frac{2}{5} + \frac{1}{5} = \frac{3}{5}$

✗ 8) $\frac{2}{3} + \frac{1}{5} = \frac{3}{15}$

✗ 3) $\frac{5}{6} + \frac{1}{2} = \frac{5}{12}$

✗ 6) $\frac{3}{7} + \frac{1}{2} = \frac{4}{14}$

✗ 9) $\frac{16}{25} + \frac{3}{5} = \frac{19}{125}$

✎ Subtract fractions.

✓ 10) $\frac{4}{5} - \frac{2}{5} = \frac{2}{5}$

✗ 13) $\frac{8}{9} - \frac{3}{5} = \frac{5}{45}$

✗ 16) $\frac{3}{4} - \frac{13}{18} = \frac{-10}{72}$

✗ 11) $\frac{3}{5} - \frac{2}{7} = \frac{1}{35}$

✗ 14) $\frac{3}{7} - \frac{3}{14} = 98$

✗ 17) $\frac{5}{8} - \frac{2}{5} = \frac{3}{45}$

✗ 12) $\frac{1}{2} - \frac{1}{3} = \frac{?}{6}$

✗ 15) $\frac{4}{15} - \frac{1}{10} = \frac{3}{150}$

✗ 18) $\frac{1}{2} - \frac{1}{9} = \frac{?}{18}$

www.EffortlessMath.com   13

Multiplying and Dividing Fractions

Helpful Hints

– **Multiplying fractions:** multiply the top numbers and multiply the bottom numbers.
– **Dividing fractions:** Keep, Change, Flip
Keep first fraction, change division sign to multiplication, and flip the numerator and denominator of the second fraction. Then, solve!

Example:
$$\frac{a}{b} \times \frac{c}{d} = \frac{a \times c}{b \times d}$$

$$\frac{a}{b} \div \frac{c}{d} = \frac{a}{b} \times \frac{d}{c} = \frac{ad}{bc}$$

✎ Multiplying fractions. Then simplify.

1) $\frac{1}{5} \times \frac{2}{3} = \frac{2}{15}$

2) $\frac{3}{4} \times \frac{2}{3} = \frac{1}{2}$

3) $\frac{2}{5} \times \frac{3}{7} = \frac{6}{35}$

4) $\frac{3}{8} \times \frac{1}{3} = \frac{1}{8}$

5) $\frac{3}{5} \times \frac{2}{5} = \frac{6}{25}$

6) $\frac{7}{9} \times \frac{1}{3} = \frac{7}{27}$

7) $\frac{2}{3} \times \frac{3}{8} = \frac{1}{4}$

8) $\frac{1}{4} \times \frac{1}{3} = \frac{1}{12}$

9) $\frac{5}{7} \times \frac{7}{12} = \frac{35}{84}$ simplify?

✎ Dividing fractions.

10) $\frac{2}{9} \div \frac{1}{4} = \frac{8}{9}$

11) $\frac{1}{2} \div \frac{1}{3} = \frac{3}{2}$

12) $\frac{6}{11} \div \frac{3}{4} = \frac{24}{33}$? simplify

13) $\frac{11}{14} \div \frac{1}{10} = \frac{14}{110}$

14) $\frac{3}{5} \div \frac{5}{9} = \frac{27}{25}$

15) $\frac{1}{2} \div \frac{1}{2} = \frac{2}{2}$ or 1

16) $\frac{3}{5} \div \frac{1}{5} = \frac{15}{5}$ simplify

17) $\frac{12}{21} \div \frac{3}{7} = \frac{84}{63}$ simplify

18) $\frac{5}{14} \div \frac{9}{10} = \frac{50}{126}$

Adding Mixed Numbers

Helpful Hints

Use the following steps for both adding and subtracting mixed numbers.

– Find the Least Common Denominator (LCD)
– Find the equivalent fractions for each mixed number.
– Add fractions after finding common denominator.
– Write your answer in lowest terms.

Example:

$1\frac{3}{4} + 2\frac{3}{8} = 4\frac{1}{8}$

✎ Add.

1) $4\frac{1}{2} + 5\frac{1}{2} = 9\frac{1}{2}$

$\frac{9}{2} + \frac{11}{2} = \frac{9+11}{2} = \frac{20}{2} = 10$

2) $2\frac{3}{8} + 3\frac{1}{8} = 5\frac{4}{8}$ or $5\frac{1}{2}$

3) $6\frac{1}{5} + 3\frac{2}{5} = 9\frac{3}{5}$

4) $1\frac{1}{3} + 2\frac{2}{3} = 4$

5) $5\frac{1}{6} + 5\frac{1}{2} = 10\frac{4}{6}$ simplify

6) $3\frac{1}{3} + 1\frac{1}{3} = 4\frac{2}{3}$

7) $1\frac{10}{11} + 1\frac{1}{3} = 2\frac{41}{33}$

8) $2\frac{3}{6} + 1\frac{1}{2} = 4$

9) $5\frac{3}{5} + 5\frac{1}{5} = 10\frac{4}{5}$

10) $7 + \frac{1}{5} = 7\frac{1}{5}$

11) $1\frac{5}{7} + \frac{1}{3} = 1\frac{22}{21}$

12) $2\frac{1}{4} + 1\frac{1}{2} = 3\frac{3}{4}$

Subtract Mixed Numbers

> **Helpful Hints**
>
> Use the following steps for both adding and subtracting mixed numbers.
>
> Find the Least Common Denominator (LCD)
> – Find the equivalent fractions for each mixed number.
> – Add or subtract fractions after finding common denominator.
> – Write your answer in lowest terms.
>
> Example:
>
> $5\frac{2}{3} - 3\frac{2}{7} = 2\frac{8}{21}$

✍ Subtract.

1) $4\frac{1}{2} - 3\frac{1}{2}$

2) $3\frac{3}{8} - 3\frac{1}{8}$

3) $6\frac{3}{5} - 5\frac{1}{5}$

4) $2\frac{1}{3} - 1\frac{2}{3}$

5) $6\frac{1}{6} - 5\frac{1}{2}$

6) $3\frac{1}{3} - 1\frac{1}{3}$

7) $2\frac{10}{11} - 1\frac{1}{3}$

8) $2\frac{1}{2} - 1\frac{1}{2}$

9) $6\frac{3}{5} - 2\frac{1}{5}$

10) $7\frac{2}{5} - 1\frac{1}{5}$

11) $2\frac{5}{7} - 1\frac{1}{3}$

12) $2\frac{1}{4} - 1\frac{1}{2}$

Multiplying Mixed Numbers

Helpful Hints

1- Convert the mixed numbers to improper fractions.
2- Multiply fractions and simplify if necessary.

$$a\frac{c}{b} = a + \frac{c}{b} = \frac{ab+c}{b}$$

Example:

$$2\frac{1}{3} \times 5\frac{3}{7} =$$

$$\frac{7}{3} \times \frac{38}{7} = \frac{38}{3} = 12\frac{2}{3}$$

✎ Find each product.

1) $1\frac{2}{3} \times 1\frac{1}{4}$

2) $1\frac{3}{5} \times 1\frac{2}{3}$

3) $1\frac{2}{3} \times 3\frac{2}{7}$

4) $4\frac{1}{8} \times 1\frac{2}{5}$

5) $2\frac{2}{5} \times 3\frac{1}{5}$

6) $1\frac{1}{3} \times 1\frac{2}{3}$

7) $1\frac{5}{8} \times 2\frac{1}{2}$

8) $3\frac{2}{5} \times 2\frac{1}{5}$

9) $2\frac{2}{3} \times 4\frac{1}{4}$

10) $2\frac{3}{5} \times 1\frac{2}{4}$

11) $1\frac{1}{3} \times 1\frac{1}{4}$

12) $3\frac{2}{5} \times 1\frac{1}{5}$

Dividing Mixed Numbers

Helpful Hints

1- Convert the mixed numbers to improper fractions.
2- Divide fractions and simplify if necessary.

$$a\frac{c}{b} = a + \frac{c}{b} = \frac{ab+c}{b}$$

Example:

$$2\frac{1}{3} \times 5\frac{3}{7} =$$

$$\frac{7}{3} \times \frac{38}{7} = \frac{38}{3} = 12\frac{2}{3}$$

✎ Find each quotient.

1) $2\frac{1}{5} \div 2\frac{1}{2}$

2) $2\frac{3}{5} \div 1\frac{1}{3}$

3) $3\frac{1}{6} \div 4\frac{2}{3}$

4) $1\frac{2}{3} \div 3\frac{1}{3}$

5) $4\frac{1}{8} \div 2\frac{2}{4}$

6) $3\frac{1}{2} \div 2\frac{3}{5}$

7) $3\frac{5}{9} \div 1\frac{2}{5}$

8) $2\frac{2}{7} \div 1\frac{1}{2}$

9) $3\frac{1}{5} \div 1\frac{1}{2}$

10) $4\frac{3}{5} \div 2\frac{1}{3}$

11) $6\frac{1}{6} \div 1\frac{2}{3}$

12) $2\frac{2}{3} \div 1\frac{1}{3}$

Comparing Decimals

> **Helpful Hints**
>
> - **Decimals:** is a fraction written in a special form. For example, instead of writing $\frac{1}{2}$ you can write 0.5.
> - **For comparing:**
>   Equal to =
>   Less than <
>   greater than >
>   greater than or equal ≥
>   Less than or equal ≤
>
> **Example:**
>
> 2.67 > 0.267

✎ **Write the correct comparison symbol (>, < or =).**

1) 1.25 2.3

2) 0.5 0.23

3) 3.2 3.2

4) 4.58 45.8

5) 2.75 0.275

6) 5.2 5

7) 3.1 0.31

8) 6.33 0.733

9) 8 0.8

10) 4.56 0.456

11) 1.12 1.14

12) 2.77 2.78

13) 6.08 6.11

14) 1.11 0.211

15) 2.6 2.55

16) 1.24 1.25

17) 5.52 0.552

18) 0.33 0.033

19) 14.4 14.4

20) 0.05 0.50

21) 0.59 0.7

22) 0.5 0.05

23) 0.90 0.9

24) 0.27 0.4

Rounding Decimals

Helpful Hints

We can round decimals to a certain accuracy or number of decimal places. This is used to make calculation easier to do and results easier to understand, when exact values are not too important.

First, you'll need to remember your place values:

Example:

6.37 = 6

12.4567

1: tens   2: ones   4: tenths

5: hundredths   6: thousandths   7: ten thousandths

✎ Round each decimal number to the nearest place indicated.

1) 0.23
2) 4.04
3) 5.623
4) 0.266
5) 6.37
6) 0.88
7) 8.24
8) 7.0760

9) 1.629
10) 6.3959
11) 1.9
12) 5.2167
13) 5.863
14) 8.54
15) 80.69
16) 65.85

17) 70.78
18) 615.755
19) 16.4
20) 95.81
21) 2.408
22) 76.3
23) 116.514
24) 8.06

Adding and Subtracting Decimals

Helpful Hints

1– Line up the numbers.

2– Add zeros to have same number of digits for both numbers.

3– Add or Subtract using column addition or subtraction.

Example:

$$\begin{array}{r} 16.18 \\ -\ 13.45 \\ \hline 2.73 \end{array}$$

✎ Add and subtract decimals.

1) $\begin{array}{r} 15.14 \\ -\ 12.18 \\ \hline \end{array}$

2) $\begin{array}{r} 65.72 \\ +\ 43.67 \\ \hline \end{array}$

3) $\begin{array}{r} 82.56 \\ +\ 12.28 \\ \hline \end{array}$

4) $\begin{array}{r} 34.18 \\ -\ 23.45 \\ \hline \end{array}$

5) $\begin{array}{r} 90.37 \\ +\ 56.97 \\ \hline \end{array}$

6) $\begin{array}{r} 45.78 \\ -\ 23.39 \\ \hline \end{array}$

✎ Solve.

7) ____ + 1.3 = 4.8

8) 4.2 + ____ = 11.6

9) 9.9 + ____ = 16

10) 6.9 + ____ = 16.4

11) ____ + 5.1 = 8.6

12) ____ + 7.9 = 15.2

Multiplying and Dividing Decimals

Helpful Hints

For Multiplication:

− Set up and multiply the numbers as you do with whole numbers.

− Count the total number of decimal places in both of the factors.

− Place the decimal point in the product.

For Division:

− If the divisor is not a whole number, move decimal point to right to make it a whole number. Do the same for dividend.

− Divide similar to whole numbers.

✎ Find each product.

1) $\begin{array}{r} 4.5 \\ \times\ 1.6 \\ \hline \end{array}$

2) $\begin{array}{r} 7.7 \\ \times\ 9.9 \\ \hline \end{array}$

3) $\begin{array}{r} 2.6 \\ \times\ 1.5 \\ \hline \end{array}$

4) $\begin{array}{r} 8.9 \\ \times\ 9.7 \\ \hline \end{array}$

5) $\begin{array}{r} 15.1 \\ \times\ 12.6 \\ \hline \end{array}$

6) $\begin{array}{r} 6.9 \\ \times\ 3.3 \\ \hline \end{array}$

7) $\begin{array}{r} 5.7 \\ \times\ 7.8 \\ \hline \end{array}$

8) $\begin{array}{r} 98.20 \\ \times\ 100 \\ \hline \end{array}$

9) $\begin{array}{r} 23.99 \\ \times\ 1000 \\ \hline \end{array}$

✎ Find each quotient.

10) $9.2 \div 3.6$

11) $27.6 \div 3.8$

12) $12.6 \div 4.7$

13) $6.5 \div 8.1$

14) $1.4 \div 10$

15) $3.6 \div 100$

16) $4.24 \div 10$

17) $14.6 \div 100$

18) $1.8 \div 1000$

Converting Between Fractions, Decimals and Mixed Numbers

Helpful Hints

Fraction to Decimal:

– Divide the top number by the bottom number.

Decimal to Fraction:

– Write decimal over 1.

– Multiply both top and bottom by 10 for every digit on the right side of the decimal point.

– Simplify.

✏ Convert fractions to decimals.

1) $\dfrac{9}{10}$ 4) $\dfrac{2}{5}$ 7) $\dfrac{12}{10}$

2) $\dfrac{56}{100}$ 5) $\dfrac{3}{9}$ 8) $\dfrac{8}{5}$

3) $\dfrac{3}{4}$ 6) $\dfrac{40}{50}$ 9) $\dfrac{69}{10}$

✏ Convert decimal into fraction or mixed numbers.

10) 0.3 14) 0.8 18) 0.08

11) 4.5 15) 0.25 19) 0.45

12) 2.5 16) 0.14 20) 2.6

13) 2.3 17) 0.2 21) 5.2

Factoring Numbers

Helpful Hints	- Factoring numbers means to break the numbers into their prime factors. - First few prime numbers: 2, 3, 5, 7, 11, 13, 17, 19	Example: $12 = 2 \times 2 \times 3$

✎ **List all positive factors of each number.**

1) 68   6) 78   11) 54

2) 56   7) 50   12) 28

3) 24   8) 98   13) 55

4) 40   9) 45   14) 85

5) 86   10) 26   15) 48

✎ **List the prime factorization for each number.**

16) 50   19) 21   22) 26

17) 25   20) 45   23) 86

18) 69   21) 68   24) 93

Greatest Common Factor

Helpful Hints

- List the prime factors of each number.
- Multiply common prime factors.

Example:

$200 = 2 \times 2 \times 2 \times 5 \times 5$

$60 = 2 \times 2 \times 3 \times 5$

GCF (200, 60) = $2 \times 2 \times 5 = 20$

✎ *Find the GCF for each number pair.*

1) 20, 30

2) 4, 14

3) 5, 45

4) 68, 12

5) 5, 12

6) 15, 27

7) 3, 24

8) 34, 6

9) 4, 10

10) 5, 3

11) 6, 16

12) 30, 3

13) 24, 28

14) 70, 10

15) 45, 8

16) 90, 35

17) 78, 34

18) 55, 75

19) 60, 72

20) 100, 78

21) 30, 40

Least Common Multiple

Helpful Hints
- Find the GCF for the two numbers.
- Divide that GCF into either number.
- Take that answer and multiply it by the other number.

Example:

LCM (200, 60):

GCF is 20

200 ÷ 20 = 10

10 × 60 = 600

✏️ *Find the LCM for each number pair.*

1) 4, 14

2) 5, 15

3) 16, 10

4) 4, 34

5) 8, 3

6) 12, 24

7) 9, 18

8) 5, 6

9) 8, 19

10) 9, 21

11) 19, 29

12) 7, 6

13) 25, 6

14) 4, 8

15) 30, 10, 50

16) 18, 36, 27

17) 12, 8, 18

18) 8, 18, 4

19) 26, 20, 30

20) 10, 4, 24

21) 15, 30, 45

Test Preparation

1) A pizza cut into 8 parts. Jason and his sister Eva ordered two pizzas. Jason ate $\frac{1}{4}$ of his pizza and Eva ate $\frac{1}{2}$ of her pizza. What part of the two pizzas was left?

   A. $\frac{1}{2}$

   B. $\frac{1}{3}$

   C. $\frac{3}{8}$

   D. $\frac{5}{8}$

2) Robert is preparing to run a marathon. He runs $7\frac{1}{5}$ miles on Saturday and two times that many on Monday and Wednesday. Robert wants to run a total of 60 miles this week. How many more miles does he need to run?

   Write your answer in the box below.

3) Last week 24,000 fans attended a football match. This week three times as many bought tickets, but one sixth of them cancelled their tickets. How many are attending this week?

   A. 48,000

   B. 54,000

   C. 60,000

   D. 72,000

4) In a bag of small balls $\frac{1}{3}$ are black, $\frac{1}{6}$ are white, $\frac{1}{4}$ are red and the remaining 12 blue. How many balls are white?

   A. 8

   B. 12

   C. 16

   D. 24

Answers of Worksheets – Chapter 1

Simplifying Fractions

1) $\frac{11}{18}$
2) $\frac{4}{5}$
3) $\frac{2}{3}$
4) $\frac{3}{4}$
5) $\frac{1}{3}$
6) $\frac{1}{4}$
7) $\frac{4}{9}$
8) $\frac{1}{2}$
9) $\frac{2}{5}$
10) $\frac{1}{9}$
11) $\frac{5}{9}$
12) $\frac{3}{4}$
13) $\frac{5}{8}$
14) $\frac{13}{16}$
15) $\frac{1}{5}$
16) $\frac{4}{7}$
17) $\frac{1}{2}$
18) $\frac{5}{12}$
19) $\frac{3}{8}$
20) $\frac{1}{4}$
21) $\frac{5}{9}$

Adding and Subtracting Fractions

1) $\frac{7}{6}$
2) $\frac{14}{15}$
3) $\frac{4}{3}$
4) $\frac{83}{36}$
5) $\frac{3}{5}$
6) $\frac{13}{14}$
7) $\frac{23}{20}$
8) $\frac{13}{15}$
9) $\frac{31}{25}$
10) $\frac{2}{5}$
11) $\frac{11}{35}$
12) $\frac{1}{6}$
13) $\frac{13}{45}$
14) $\frac{3}{14}$
15) $\frac{1}{6}$
16) $\frac{1}{36}$
17) $\frac{9}{40}$
18) $\frac{7}{18}$

Multiplying and Dividing Fractions

1) $\frac{2}{15}$
2) $\frac{1}{2}$
3) $\frac{6}{35}$
4) $\frac{1}{8}$
5) $\frac{6}{25}$
6) $\frac{7}{27}$
7) $\frac{1}{4}$
8) $\frac{1}{12}$
9) $\frac{5}{12}$
10) $\frac{8}{9}$
11) $\frac{3}{2}$
12) $\frac{8}{11}$
13) $\frac{55}{7}$
14) $\frac{27}{25}$
15) 1
16) 3
17) $\frac{4}{3}$
18) $\frac{25}{63}$

Adding Mixed Numbers

1) 10
2) $5\frac{1}{2}$
3) $9\frac{3}{5}$
4) 4
5) $10\frac{2}{3}$
6) $4\frac{2}{3}$
7) $3\frac{8}{33}$
8) 4
9) $10\frac{4}{5}$
10) $7\frac{1}{5}$
11) $2\frac{1}{21}$
12) $3\frac{3}{4}$

Subtract Mixed Numbers

1) 1
2) $\frac{1}{4}$
3) $1\frac{2}{5}$
4) $\frac{2}{3}$
5) $\frac{2}{3}$
6) 2
7) $1\frac{19}{33}$
8) 1
9) $4\frac{2}{5}$
10) $6\frac{1}{5}$
11) $1\frac{8}{21}$
12) $\frac{3}{4}$

Multiplying Mixed Numbers

1) $2\frac{1}{12}$
2) $2\frac{2}{3}$
3) $5\frac{10}{21}$
4) $5\frac{31}{40}$

5) $7\frac{17}{25}$
6) $2\frac{2}{9}$
7) $4\frac{1}{16}$
8) $7\frac{12}{25}$

9) $11\frac{1}{3}$
10) $3\frac{9}{10}$
11) $1\frac{2}{3}$
12) $4\frac{2}{25}$

Dividing Mixed Numbers

1) $\frac{22}{25}$
2) $1\frac{19}{20}$
3) $\frac{19}{28}$
4) $\frac{1}{2}$

5) $1\frac{13}{20}$
6) $1\frac{9}{26}$
7) $2\frac{34}{63}$
8) $1\frac{11}{21}$

9) $2\frac{2}{15}$
10) $1\frac{34}{35}$
11) $3\frac{7}{10}$
12) 2

Comparing Decimals

1) 1.25 < 2.3
2) 0.5 > 0.23
3) 3.2 = 3.2
4) 4.58 < 45.8
5) 2.75 > 0.275
6) 5.2 > 5
7) 3.1 > 0.31
8) 6.33 > 0.733
9) 8 > 0.8
10) 4.56 > 0.456
11) 1.12 < 1.14
12) 2.77 < 2.78

13) 6.08 < 6.11
14) 1.11 > 0.211
15) 2.6 > 2.55
16) 1.24 < 1.25
17) 5.52 > 0.552
18) 0.33 > 0.033
19) 14.4 = 14.4
20) 0.05 < 0.50
21) 0.59 < 0.7
22) 0.5 > 0.05
23) 0.90 = 0.9
24) 0.27 < 0.4

Rounding Decimals

1) 0.2	9) 1.63	17) 70.8
2) 4.0	10) 6.4	18) 616
3) 5.6	11) 2	19) 16
4) 0.3	12) 5	20) 96
5) 6	13) 5.9	21) 2
6) 0.9	14) 8.5	22) 76
7) 8.2	15) 81	23) 116.5
8) 7	16) 66	24) 8.1

Adding and Subtracting Decimals

1) 2.96	5) 147.34	9) 6.1
2) 109.39	6) 22.39	10) 9.5
3) 94.84	7) 3.5	11) 3.5
4) 10.73	8) 7.4	12) 7.3

Multiplying and Dividing Decimals

1) 7.2	7) 44.46	13) 0.8024...
2) 76.23	8) 9820	14) 0.14
3) 3.9	9) 23990	15) 0.036
4) 86.33	10) 2.5555...	16) 0.424
5) 190.26	11) 7.2631...	17) 0.146
6) 22.77	12) 2.6808...	18) 0.0018

Converting Between Fractions, Decimals and Mixed Numbers

1) 0.9	7) 1.2	12) $2\frac{1}{2}$
2) 0.56	8) 1.6	13) $2\frac{3}{10}$
3) 0.75	9) 6.9	
4) 0.4	10) $\frac{3}{10}$	14) $\frac{4}{5}$
5) 0.333...		15) $\frac{1}{4}$
6) 0.8	11) $4\frac{1}{2}$	

16) $\frac{7}{50}$ 18) $\frac{2}{25}$ 20) $2\frac{3}{5}$

17) $\frac{1}{5}$ 19) $\frac{9}{20}$ 21) $5\frac{1}{5}$

Factoring Numbers

1) 1, 2, 4, 17, 34, 68
2) 1, 2, 4, 7, 8, 14, 28, 56
3) 1, 2, 3, 4, 6, 8, 12, 24
4) 1, 2, 4, 5, 8, 10, 20, 40
5) 1, 2, 43, 86
6) 1, 2, 3, 6, 13, 26, 39, 78
7) 1, 2, 5, 10, 25, 50
8) 1, 2, 7, 14, 49, 98
9) 1, 3, 5, 9, 15, 45
10) 1, 2, 13, 26
11) 1, 2, 3, 6, 9, 18, 27, 54
12) 1, 2, 4, 7, 14, 28
13) 1, 5, 11, 55
14) 1, 5, 17, 85
15) 1, 2, 3, 4, 6, 8, 12, 16, 24, 48
16) $2 \times 5 \times 5$
17) 5×5
18) 3×23
19) 3×7
20) $3 \times 3 \times 5$
21) $2 \times 2 \times 17$
22) 2×13
23) 2×43
24) 3×31

Greatest Common Factor

1) 10
2) 2
3) 5
4) 4
5) 1
6) 3
7) 3
8) 2
9) 2
10) 1
11) 2
12) 3
13) 4
14) 10
15) 1
16) 5
17) 2
18) 5
19) 12
20) 2
21) 10

Least Common Multiple

1) 28
2) 15
3) 80
4) 68
5) 24
6) 24
7) 18
8) 30
9) 152
10) 63
11) 551
12) 42
13) 150
14) 8
15) 150
16) 108
17) 72
18) 72
19) 780
20) 120
21) 90

Test Preparation Answers

1) Choice D is correct

Jason ate $\frac{1}{4}$ of 8 parts of his pizza. It means 2 parts out of 8 parts ($\frac{1}{4}$ of 8 parts = $x \Rightarrow x = 2$) and left 6 parts.

Eva ate $\frac{1}{2}$ of 8 parts of her pizza. It means 4 parts out of 8 parts ($\frac{1}{2}$ of 8 parts = $x \Rightarrow x = 4$) and left 4 parts.

Therefore, they ate (4 + 2) parts out of (8+8) parts of their pizza and left (6 + 4) parts out of (8+8) parts of their pizza that equals to: $\frac{10}{16}$

After simplification, the answer is: $\frac{5}{8}$

2) The answer is $38\frac{2}{5}$ miles.

Robert runs $7\frac{1}{5}$ miles on Saturday and $2 \times (7\frac{1}{5})$ miles on Monday and Wednesday.
Robert wants to run a total of 60 miles this week.
Therefore, $7\frac{1}{5} + 2 \times (7\frac{1}{5})$ should be subtracted from 60:
$60 - (7\frac{1}{5} + 2(7\frac{1}{5})) = 60 - 21\frac{3}{5} = 38\frac{2}{5}$ miles

3) Choice C is correct

Three times of 24,000 is 72,000. One sixth of them cancelled their tickets.

One sixth of 72,000 equals 12,000. ($1/6 \times 72000 = 12000$).

60,000 (72000 − 12000 = 60000) fans are attending this week

4) **Choice A is correct**

Let x be the total number of balls. Then:

$\frac{1}{3}x + \frac{1}{6}x + \frac{1}{4}x + 12 = x$

$$\left(\frac{1}{3} + \frac{1}{6} + \frac{1}{4}\right)x + 12 = x$$

$(\frac{9}{12})x + 12 = x \rightarrow 12 = x - \frac{3}{4}x = \frac{1}{4}x$

$\frac{1}{4}x$ equals 12. Then:

$\frac{1}{4}x = 12 \rightarrow x = 48$

x is the total number of balls. Therefore, number of white balls is:

$$\frac{1}{6}x = \frac{1}{6} \times 48 = 8$$

Chapter 2: Real Numbers and Integers

Topics that you'll learn in this chapter:

- ✓ Adding and Subtracting Integers
- ✓ Multiplying and Dividing Integers
- ✓ Ordering Integers and Numbers
- ✓ Arrange and Order, Comparing Integers
- ✓ Order of Operations
- ✓ Mixed Integer Computations
- ✓ Integers and Absolute Value

Adding and Subtracting Integers

Helpful Hints

- **Integers:** {... , −3, −2, −1, 0, 1, 2, 3, ...}
  Includes: zero, counting numbers, and the negative of the counting numbers.
- Add a positive integer by moving to the right on the number line.
- Add a negative integer by moving to the left on the number line.
- Subtract an integer by adding its opposite.

Example:

$12 + 10 = 22$

$25 − 13 = 12$

$(−24) + 12 = −12$

$(−14) + (−12) = −26$

$14 − (−13) = 27$

✎ **Find the sum.**

1) $(−12) + (−4)$

2) $5 + (−24)$

3) $(−14) + 23$

4) $(−8) + (39)$

5) $43 + (−12)$

6) $(−23) + (−4) + 3$

7) $4 + (−12) + (−10) + (−25)$

8) $19 + (−15) + 25 + 11$

9) $(−9) + (−12) + (32 − 14)$

10) $4 + (−30) + (45 − 34)$

✎ **Find the difference.**

11) $(−14) − (−9) − (18)$

12) $(−9) − (−25)$

13) $(−12) − (8)$

14) $(28) − (−4)$

15) $(34) − (2)$

16) $(55) − (−5) + (−4)$

17) $(9) − (2) − (−5)$

18) $(2) − (4) − (−15)$

19) $(23) − (4) − (−34)$

20) $(−45) − (−87)$

Multiplying and Dividing Integers

Helpful Hints

(negative) × (negative) = positive

(negative) ÷ (negative) = positive

(negative) × (positive) = negative

(negative) ÷ (positive) = negative

(positive) × (positive) = positive

Examples:

$3 \times 2 = 6$

$3 \times -3 = -9$

$-2 \times -2 = 4$

$10 \div 2 = 5$

$-4 \div 2 = -2$

$-12 \div -6 = 3$

✎ Find each product.

1) $(-8) \times (-2)$

2) 3×6

3) $(-4) \times 5 \times (-6)$

4) $2 \times (-6) \times (-6)$

5) $11 \times (-12)$

6) $10 \times (-5)$

7) 8×8

8) $(-8) \times (-9)$

9) $6 \times (-5) \times 3$

10) $6 \times (-1) \times 2$

✎ Find each quotient.

11) $18 \div 3$

12) $(-24) \div 4$

13) $(-63) \div (-9)$

14) $54 \div 9$

15) $20 \div (-2)$

16) $(-66) \div (-11)$

17) $64 \div 8$

18) $(-121) \div 11$

19) $72 \div 9$

20) $16 \div 4$

Ordering Integers and Numbers

Helpful Hints

To compare numbers, you can use number line! as you move from left to right on the number line, you find a bigger number!

Example:

Order integers from least to greatest.

$(-11, -13, 7, -2, 12)$

$-13 < -11 < -2 < 7 < 12$

✎ *Order each set of integers from least to greatest.*

1) $-15, -19, 20, -4, 1$ ___, ___, ___, ___, ___, ___

2) $6, -5, 4, -3, 2$ ___, ___, ___, ___, ___, ___

3) $15, -42, 19, 0, -22$ ___, ___, ___, ___, ___, ___

4) $26, -91, 0, -13, 67, -55$ ___, ___, ___, ___, ___, ___

5) $-17, -71, 90, -25, -54, -39$ ___, ___, ___, ___, ___, ___

6) $98, 5, 46, 19, 77, 24$ ___, ___, ___, ___, ___, ___

✎ *Order each set of integers from greatest to least.*

7) $-2, 5, -3, 6, -4$ ___, ___, ___, ___, ___, ___

8) $-37, 7, -17, 27, 47$ ___, ___, ___, ___, ___, ___

9) $32, -27, 19, -17, 15$ ___, ___, ___, ___, ___, ___

10) $68, 81, 21, -18, 94, 72$ ___, ___, ___, ___, ___, ___

Arrange, Order, and Comparing Integers

Helpful Hints

When using a number line, numbers increase as you move to the right.

Examples:

$5 < 7$,

$-5 < -2$

$-18 < -12$

✎ *Arrange these integers in descending order.*

1) 21, 71, −18, −10, 82   ___, ___, ___, ___, ___

2) 15, 11, 20, 12, −9, −5   ___, ___, ___, ___, ___, ___

3) −5, 20, 15, 9, −11   ___, ___, ___, ___, ___

4) 19, 18, −9, −6, −11   ___, ___, ___, ___, ___

5) 56, −34, −12, −5, 32   ___, ___, ___, ___, ___

✎ *Compare. Use >, =, <*

6) −8 ____ 12

7) −10 ____ −16

8) 43 ____ 34

9) 15 ____ −16

10) −354 ____ −345

11) −56 ____ −58

12) 78 ____ 87

13) −92 ____ −102

14) −12 ____ −12

15) −721 ____ −821

Order of Operations

Helpful Hints
- Use "order of operations" rule when there are more than one math operation.
- PEMDAS
  (parentheses / exponents / multiply / divide / add / subtract)

Example:

$(12 + 4) \div (-4) = -4$

✎ *Evaluate each expression.*

1) $(2 \times 2) + 5$

2) $24 - (3 \times 3)$

3) $(6 \times 4) + 8$

4) $25 - (4 \times 2)$

5) $(6 \times 5) + 3$

6) $64 - (2 \times 4)$

7) $25 + (1 \times 8)$

8) $(6 \times 7) + 7$

9) $48 \div (4 + 4)$

10) $(7 + 11) \div (-2)$

11) $9 + (2 \times 5) + 10$

12) $(5 + 8) \times \frac{3}{5} + 2$

13) $2 \times 7 - (\frac{10}{9 - 4})$

14) $(12 + 2 - 5) \times 7 - 1$

15) $(\frac{7}{5 - 1}) \times (2 + 6) \times 2$

16) $20 \div (4 - (10 - 8))$

17) $\frac{50}{4(5 - 4) - 3}$

18) $2 + (8 \times 2)$

www.EffortlessMath.com

Mixed Integer Computations

Helpful Hints	It worth remembering: (negative) × (negative) = positive (negative) ÷ (negative) = positive (negative) × (positive) = negative (negative) ÷ (positive) = negative (positive) × (positive) = positive	Example: (−5) + 6 = 1 (−3) × (−2) = 6 (9) ÷ (−3) = −3

✏️ *Compute.*

1) $(-70) \div (-5)$

2) $(-14) \times 3$

3) $(-4) \times (-15)$

4) $(-65) \div 5$

5) $18 \times (-7)$

6) $(-12) \times (-2)$

7) $\dfrac{(-60)}{(-20)}$

8) $24 \div (-8)$

9) $22 \div (-11)$

10) $\dfrac{(-27)}{3}$

11) $4 \times (-4)$

12) $\dfrac{(-48)}{12}$

13) $(-14) \times (-2)$

14) $(-7) \times (7)$

15) $\dfrac{-30}{-6}$

16) $(-54) \div 6$

17) $(-60) \div (-5)$

18) $(-7) \times (-12)$

19) $(-14) \times 5$

20) $88 \div (-8)$

Integers and Absolute Value

Helpful Hints

To find an absolute value of a number, just find it's distance from 0!

Example:

$|-6| = 6$

$|6| = 6$

$|-12| = 12$

$|12| = 12$

✎ Write absolute value of each number.

1) -4
2) -7
3) -8
4) 4
5) 5
6) -10
7) 1
8) 6
9) 8
10) -2
11) -1
12) 10
13) 3
14) 7
15) -5
16) -3
17) -9
18) 2
19) 4
20) -6
21) 9

✎ Evaluate.

22) $|-43| - |12| + 10$

23) $76 + |-15 - 45| - |3|$

24) $30 + |-62| - 46$

25) $|32| - |-78| + 90$

26) $|-35 + 4| + 6 - 4$

27) $|-4| + |-11|$

28) $|-6 + 3 - 4| + |7 + 7|$

29) $|-9| + |-19| - 5$

Test Preparation

1) 5 less than twice a positive integer is 83. What is the integer?

   A. 39

   B. 41

   C. 42

   D. 44

2) $[6 \times (-24) + 8] - (-4) + [4 \times 5] \div 2 = ?$

   Write your answer in the box below.

   ☐

3) Three times the price of a laptop is equal to five times the price of a computer. If the price of laptop is $200 more than the computer, what is the price of the laptop?

   A. 300

   B. 500

   C. 800

   D. 1500

4) Two numbers are shown on the number line.

$$\frac{\sqrt{16}}{4} \qquad 3\pi$$

Which value is NOT located between these two numbers?

A. $\dfrac{3\pi}{4}$

B. $\dfrac{\pi}{2}$

C. $\sqrt{16}$

D. $\dfrac{3\pi}{16}$

Answers of Worksheets – Chapter 2

Adding and Subtracting Integers

1) − 16
2) − 19
3) 9
4) 31
5) 31
6) − 24
7) − 43
8) 40
9) − 3
10) − 15
11) − 23
12) 16
13) − 20
14) 32
15) 32
16) 56
17) 12
18) 13
19) 53
20) 42

Multiplying and Dividing Integers

1) 16
2) 18
3) 120
4) 72
5) − 132
6) − 50
7) 64
8) 72
9) − 90
10) − 12
11) 6
12) − 6
13) 7
14) 6
15) − 10
16) 6
17) 8
18) − 11
19) 8
20) 4

Ordering Integers and Numbers

1) − 19, − 15, − 4, 1, 20
2) − 5, − 3, 2, 4, 6
3) − 42, − 22, 0, 15, 19
4) − 91, − 55, − 13, 0, 26, 67
5) − 71, − 54, − 39, − 25, − 17, 90
6) 5, 19, 24, 46, 77, 98
7) 6, 5, − 2, − 3, − 4
8) 47, 27, 7, − 17, − 37
9) 32, 19, 15, − 17, − 27
10) 94, 81, 72, 68, 21, − 18

Arrange and Order, Comparing Integers

1) 82, 71, 21, − 10, − 18
2) 20, 15, 12, 11, − 5, − 9
3) 20, 15, 9, − 5, −11
4) 19, 18, − 6, − 9, − 11
5) 56, 32, − 5, − 12, − 34

6) <
7) >
8) >
9) >

10) <
11) >
12) <
13) >

14) =
15) >

Order of Operations

1) 9
2) 15
3) 32
4) 17
5) 33
6) 56

7) 33
8) 49
9) 6
10) − 9
11) 29
12) 9.8

13) 12
14) 62
15) 28
16) 10
17) 50
18) 18

Mixed Integer Computations

1) 14
2) − 42
3) 60
4) − 13
5) − 126
6) 24
7) 3

8) − 3
9) − 2
10) − 9
11) − 16
12) − 4
13) 28
14) − 49

15) 5
16) − 9
17) 12
18) 84
19) − 70
20) − 11

Integers and Absolute Value

1) 4	11) 1	21) 9
2) 7	12) 10	22) 41
3) 8	13) 3	23) 133
4) 4	14) 7	24) 46
5) 5	15) 5	25) 44
6) 10	16) 3	26) 33
7) 1	17) 9	27) 15
8) 6	18) 2	28) 21
9) 8	19) 4	29) 23
10) 2	20) 6	

Test Preparation Answers

1) Choice D is correct

Let x be the integer. Then:

$2x - 5 = 83$

Add 5 both sides: $2x = 88$

Divide both sides by 2: $x = 44$

2) The answer is: − 122

Use PEMDAS (order of operation):

$[6 \times (-24) + 8] - (-4) + [4 \times 5] \div 2 = [-144 + 8] - (-4) + [20] \div 2 =$

$[-144 + 8] - (-4) + 10 =$

$[-136] - (-4) + 10 = [-136] + 4 + 10 = -122$

3) Choice B is correct

Let L be the price of laptop and C be the price of computer.

$3(L) = 5(C)$ and $L = \$200 + C$

Therefore, $3(\$200 + C) = 5C \Rightarrow \$600 + 3C = 5C \Rightarrow C = \$300$

$L = \$200 + C = \$200 + \$300 = \$500$

4) Choice D is correct.

$\frac{\sqrt{16}}{4} = 1$ and 3π is little more than 9

Alternative A is more than 1 and less than 3π ($1 < \frac{3\pi}{4} < 3\pi$).

Alternative B is more than 1 and less than 3π ($1 < \frac{\pi}{2} < 3\pi$).

Alternative C is more than 1 and less than 3π ($1 < 4 < 3\pi$).

But alternative D is not between 1 and 3π ($\frac{3\pi}{16} = 0.58$).

Chapter 3: Proportions and Ratios

Math Topics that you'll learn today:

- ✓ Writing Ratios
- ✓ Simplifying Ratios
- ✓ Proportional Ratios
- ✓ Create a Proportion
- ✓ Similar Figures
- ✓ Similar Figure Word Problems
- ✓ Ratio and Rates Word Problems

Writing Ratios

Helpful Hints
— A ratio is a comparison of two numbers. Ratio can be written as a division.

Example:

$3 : 5$, or $\dfrac{3}{5}$

✎ *Express each ratio as a rate and unite rate.*

1) 120 miles on 4 gallons of gas.

2) 24 dollars for 6 books.

3) 200 miles on 14 gallons of gas

4) 24 inches of snow in 8 hours

✎ *Express each ratio as a fraction in the simplest form.*

5) 3 feet out of 30 feet

6) 18 cakes out of 42 cakes

7) 16 dimes t0 24 dimes

8) 12 dimes out of 48 coins

9) 14 cups to 84 cups

10) 45 gallons to 65 gallons

11) 10 miles out of 40 miles

12) 22 blue cars out of 55 cars

13) 32 pennies to 300 pennies

14) 24 beetles out of 86 insects

Simplifying Ratios

Helpful *Hints*	– You can calculate equivalent ratios by multiplying or dividing both sides of the ratio by the same number.	**Examples:** 3 : 6 = 1 : 2 4 : 9 = 8 : 18

✏️ **Reduce each ratio.**

1) 21 : 49

2) 20 : 40

3) 10 : 50

4) 14 : 18

5) 45 : 27

6) 49 : 21

7) 100 : 10

8) 12 : 8

9) 35 : 45

10) 8 : 20

11) 25 : 35

12) 21 : 27

13) 52 : 82

14) 12 : 36

15) 24 : 3

16) 15 : 30

17) 3 : 36

18) 8 : 16

19) 6 : 100

20) 2 : 20

21) 10 : 60

22) 14 : 63

23) 68 : 80

24) 8 : 80

Create a Proportion

Helpful Hints

– A proportion contains 2 equal fractions! A proportion simply means that two fractions are equal.

Example:

2, 4, 8, 16

$$\frac{2}{4} = \frac{8}{16}$$

✍ Create proportion from the given set of numbers.

1) 1, 6, 2, 3

2) 12, 144, 1, 12

3) 16, 4, 8, 2

4) 9, 5, 27, 15

5) 7, 10, 60, 42

6) 8, 7, 24, 21

7) 10, 5, 8, 4

8) 3, 12, 8, 2

9) 2, 2, 1, 4

10) 3, 6, 7, 14

11) 2, 6, 5, 15

12) 7, 2, 14, 4

Similar Figures

Helpful Hints

– Two or more figures are similar if the corresponding angles are equal, and the corresponding sides are in proportion.

Example:

3–4–5 triangle is similar to a

6–8–10 triangle

✎ *Each pair of figures is similar. Find the missing side.*

1)

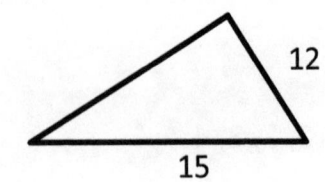

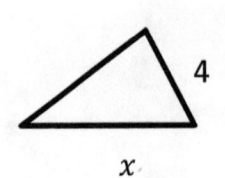

   Triangle with sides 15 and 12; similar triangle with sides x and 4.

2)

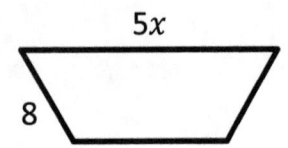

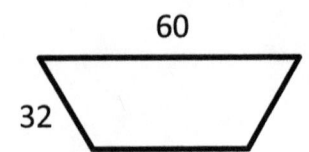

   Trapezoid with sides $5x$ and 8; similar trapezoid with sides 60 and 32.

3)

   Rectangle with sides 40 and 56, missing side x; similar rectangle with sides 7, 5, 7, 5.

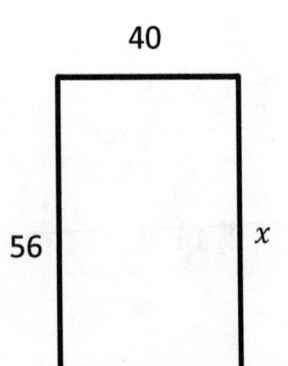

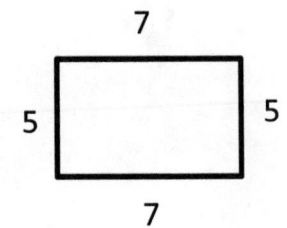

Simple Interest

> **Helpful Hints**
>
> **Simple Interest:** The charge for borrowing money or the return for lending it.
> Interest = principal × rate × time
>
> $$I = prt$$
>
> **Example:**
>
> $450 at 7% for 8 years.
>
> $$I = prt$$
>
> $$I = 450 \times 0.07 \times 8 = \$252 =$$

✎ *Use simple interest to find the ending balance.*

1) $1,300 at 5% for 6 years.

2) $5,400 at 7.5% for 6 months.

3) $25,600 at 9.2% for 5 years

4) $24,000 at 8.5% for 9 years.

5) $450 at 7% for 8 years.

6) $54,200 at 8% for 5 years.

7) $240 interest is earned on a principal of $1500 at a simple interest rate of 4% interest per year. For how many years was the principal invested?

8) A new car, valued at $28,000, depreciates at 9% per year from original price. Find the value of the car 3 years after purchase.

9) Sara puts $2,000 into an investment yielding 5% annual simple interest; she left the money in for five years. How much interest does Sara get at the end of those five years?

Ratio and Rates Word Problems

> **Helpful Hints**
>
> To solve a ratio or a rate word problem, create a proportion and use cross multiplication method!
>
> **Example:**
>
> $\dfrac{x}{4} = \dfrac{8}{16}$
>
> $16x = 4 \times 8$
>
> $x = 2$

Solve.

1) In a party, 10 soft drinks are required for every 12 guests. If there are 252 guests, how many soft drink is required?

2) In Jack's class, 18 of the students are tall and 10 are short. In Michael's class 54 students are tall and 30 students are short. Which class has a higher ratio of tall to short students?

3) Are these ratios equivalent?

    12 cards to 72 animals 11 marbles to 66 marbles

4) The price of 3 apples at the Quick Market is $1.44. The price of 5 of the same apples at Walmart is $2.50. Which place is the better buy?

5) The bakers at a Bakery can make 160 bagels in 4 hours. How many bagels can they bake in 16 hours? What is that rate per hour?

6) You can buy 5 cans of green beans at a supermarket for $3.40. How much does it cost to buy 35 cans of green beans?

Test Preparation

1) A girl 160 cm tall, stands 360 cm from a lamp post at night. Her shadow from the light is 90 cm long. How high is the lamp post?

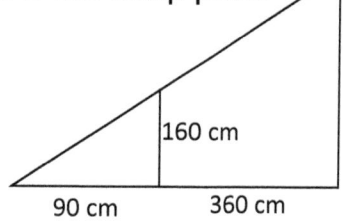

Write your answer in the box below.

2) If a tree casts a 24-foot shadow at the same time that a yardstick casts a 2-foot shadow, what is the height of the tree?

A. 24 ft
B. 28 ft
C. 36 ft
D. 48 ft

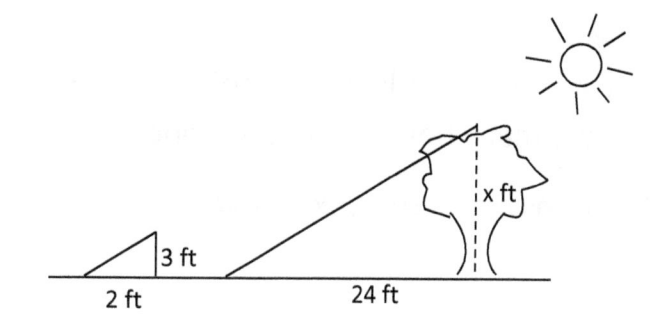

3) John traveled 150 km in 6 hours and Alice traveled 180 km in 4 hours. What is the ratio of the average speed of John to average speed of Alice?

A. 3 : 2

B. 2 : 3

C. 5 : 9

D. 5 : 6

4) The following trapezoid are similar. What is the value of x ?

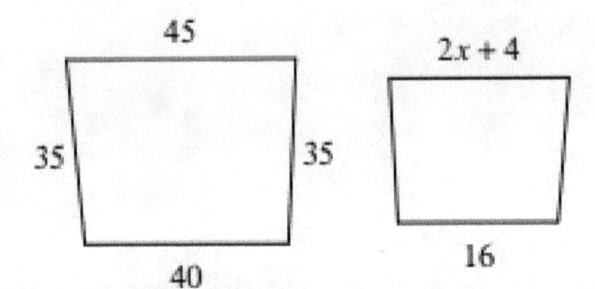

A. 7

B. 8

C. 18

D. 45

5) The ratio of boys to girls in a school is 5:3. If there are 640 students in a school, how many boys are in the school.

Write your answer in the box below.

Answers of Worksheets – Chapter 3

Writing Ratios

1) $\frac{120 \text{ miles}}{4 \text{ gallons}}$, 30 miles per gallon

2) $\frac{24 \text{ dollars}}{6 \text{ books}}$, 4.00 dollars per book

3) $\frac{200 \text{ miles}}{14 \text{ gallons}}$, 14.29 miles per gallon

4) $\frac{24" \text{ of snow}}{8 \text{ hours}}$, 3 inches of snow per hour

5) $\frac{1}{10}$ 9) $\frac{1}{6}$ 13) $\frac{8}{75}$

6) $\frac{3}{7}$ 10) $\frac{9}{13}$ 14) $\frac{12}{43}$

7) $\frac{2}{3}$ 11) $\frac{1}{4}$

8) $\frac{1}{4}$ 12) $\frac{2}{5}$

Simplifying Ratios

1) 3 : 7   9) 7 : 9   17) 1 : 12
2) 1 : 2   10) 2 : 5   18) 1 : 2
3) 1 : 5   11) 5 : 7   19) 3 : 50
4) 7 : 9   12) 7 : 9   20) 1 : 10
5) 5 : 3   13) 26 : 41   21) 1 : 6
6) 7 : 3   14) 1 : 3   22) 2 : 9
7) 10 : 1   15) 8 : 1   23) 17 : 20
8) 3 : 2   16) 1 : 2   24) 1 : 10

Create a Proportion

1) 1 : 3 = 2 : 6   5) 7 : 42, 10 : 60   9) 4 : 2 = 2 : 1
2) 12 : 144 = 1 : 12   6) 7 : 21 = 8 : 24   10) 7 : 3 = 14 : 6
3) 2 : 4 = 8 : 16   7) 8 : 10 = 4 : 5   11) 5 : 2 = 15 : 6
4) 5 : 15 = 9 : 27   8) 2 : 3 = 8 : 12   12) 7 : 2 = 14 : 4

Similar Figures

1) 5

2) 3

3) 56

Simple Interest

1) $1,690.00

2) $5,602.50

3) $37,376.00

4) $42,360.00

5) $702.00

6) $75,880.00

7) 4 years

8) $20,440

9) $500

Ratio and Rates Word Problems

1) 210

2) The ratio for both class is equal to 9 to 5.

3) Yes! Both ratios are 1 to 6

4) The price at the Quick Market is a better buy.

5) 640, the rate is 40 per hour.

6) $23.80

Test Preparation Answers

1) The answer is 800 cm.

Write the proportion and solve for missing side.

$\dfrac{\text{Smaller triangle height}}{\text{Smaller triangle base}} = \dfrac{\text{Bigger triangle height}}{\text{Bigger triangle base}} \Rightarrow \dfrac{90cm}{160cm} = \dfrac{90+360cm}{x} \Rightarrow x = 800\ cm$

2) Choice C is correct.

Write the proportion and solve.

$\dfrac{3ft}{2ft} = \dfrac{x}{24ft} \Rightarrow x = 36\ ft$

3) Choice C is correct

The average speed of John is: 150 ÷ 6 = 25 km

The average speed of Alice is: 180 ÷ 4 = 45 km

Write the ratio and simplify.

25 : 45 ⇒ 5 : 9

4) Choice A is correct

Write a proportion and solve for x.

$\dfrac{45}{40} = \dfrac{2x+4}{16} \Rightarrow 40(2x+4) = 45 \times 16 \Rightarrow 80x + 160 = 720 \Rightarrow 80x = 560 \Rightarrow x = 7$

5) The correct answer is 400.

The ratio of boys to girls is 5:3. Therefore, there are 5 boys out of 8 students. To find the answer, first divide the total number of students by 8, then multiply the result by 5.

$640 \div 8 = 80 \Rightarrow 80 \times 5 = 400$

Chapter 4: Percent

Math Topics that you'll learn today:

- ✓ Percentage Calculations
- ✓ Converting Between Percent, Fractions, and Decimals
- ✓ Percent Problems
- ✓ Find What Percentage a Number Is of Another
- ✓ Find a Percentage of a Given Number
- ✓ Percent of Increase and Decrease
- ✓ Markup, Discount, and Tax

Percentage Calculations

> **Helpful Hints** - Use the following formula to find part, whole, or percent:
>
> $\text{part} = \dfrac{\text{percent}}{100} \times \text{whole}$
>
> **Example:**
>
> $\dfrac{20}{100} \times 100 = 20$

✎ **Calculate the percentages.**

1) 50% of 25
2) 80% of 15
3) 30% of 34
4) 70% of 45
5) 10% of 0
6) 80% of 22

7) 65% of 8
8) 78% of 54
9) 50% of 80
10) 20% of 10
11) 40% of 40
12) 90% of 0

13) 20% of 70
14) 55% of 60
15) 80% of 10
16) 20% of 880
17) 70% of 100
18) 80% of 90

✎ **Solve.**

19) 50 is what percentage of 75?

20) What percentage of 100 is 70

21) Find what percentage of 60 is 35.

22) 40 is what percentage of 80?

Converting Between Percent, Fractions, and Decimals

Helpful Hints

– To a percent: Move the decimal point 2 places to the right and add the % symbol.

– Divide by 100 to convert a number from percent to decimal.

Examples:

30% = 0.3

0.24 = 24%

✎ *Converting fractions to decimals.*

1) $\dfrac{50}{100}$

2) $\dfrac{38}{100}$

3) $\dfrac{15}{100}$

4) $\dfrac{80}{100}$

5) $\dfrac{7}{100}$

6) $\dfrac{35}{100}$

7) $\dfrac{90}{100}$

8) $\dfrac{20}{100}$

9) $\dfrac{7}{100}$

✎ *Write each decimal as a percent.*

10) 0.5

11) 0.9

12) 0.002

13) 0.524

14) 0.1

15) 0.03

16) 3.63

17) 0.008

18) 4.78

Percent Problems

Helpful Hints	Base = Part ÷ Percent Part = Percent × Base Percent = Part ÷ Base	Example: 2 is 10% of 20. 2 ÷ 0.10 = 20 2 = 0.10 × 20 0.10 = 2 ÷ 20

Solve each problem.

1) 51 is 340% of what?

2) 93% of what number is 97?

3) 27% of 142 is what number?

4) What percent of 125 is 29.3?

5) 60 is what percent of 126?

6) 67 is 67% of what?

7) 67 is 13% of what?

8) 41% of 78 is what?

9) 1 is what percent of 52.6?

10) What is 59% of 14 m?

11) What is 90% of 130 inches?

12) 16 inches is 35% of what?

13) 90% of 54.4 hours is what?

14) What percent of 33.5 is 21?

15) Liam scored 22 out of 30 marks in Algebra, 35 out of 40 marks in science and 89 out of 100 marks in mathematics. In which subject his percentage of marks in best?

16) Ella require 50% to pass. If she gets 280 marks and falls short by 20 marks, what were the maximum marks she could have got?

Find What Percentage a Number Is of Another

Helpful Hints

PERCENT: the number with the percent sign (%).
PART: the number with the word "is".
WHOLE: the number with the word "of".
– Divide the Part by the Base.
– Convert the answer to percent.

Example:
20 is what percent of 50?
20 ÷ 50 = 0.40 = 40%

Find the percentage of the numbers.

1) 5 is what percent of 90?

2) 15 is what percent of 75?

3) 20 is what percent of 400?

4) 18 is what percent of 90?

5) 3 is what percent of 15?

6) 8 is what percent of 80?

7) 11 is what percent of 55?

8) 9 is what percent of 90?

9) 2.5 is what percent of 10?

10) 5 is what percent of 25?

11) 60 is what percent of 20?

12) 12 is what percent of 48?

13) 14 is what percent of 28?

14) 8.2 is what percent of 32.8?

15) 1200 is what percent of 4,800?

16) 4,000 is what percent of 20,000?

17) 45 is what percent of 900?

18) 10 is what percent of 200?

19) 15 is what percent of 60?

20) 1.2 is what percent of 24?

Find a Percentage of a Given Number

> *Helpful Hints* — Use following formula to find part, whole, or percent:
> $$\text{part} = \frac{\text{percent}}{100} \times \text{whole}$$
>
> **Example:**
> $\frac{50}{100} \times 50 = 25$

Find a Percentage of a Given Number.

1) 90% of 50

2) 40% of 50

3) 10% of 0

4) 80% of 80

5) 60% of 40

6) 50% of 60

7) 30% of 20

8) 35% of 10

9) 10% of 80

10) 10% of 60

11) 100% 0f 50

12) 90% of 34

13) 80% of 42

14) 90% of 12

15) 20% of 56

16) 40% of 40

17) 40% of 6

18) 70% of 38

19) 30% of 3

20) 40% of 50

21) 100% of 8

Percent of Increase and Decrease

Helpful Hints

– To find the percentage increase:
New Number – Original Number
The result ÷ Original Number × 100
If your answer is a negative number, then this is a percentage decrease.

To calculate percentage decrease:
Original Number – New Number
The result ÷ Original Number × 100

Example:
From 84 miles to 24 miles = 71.43% decrease

✍ *Find each percent change to the nearest percent. Increase or decrease.*

1) From 32 grams to 82 grams.

2) From 150 m to 45 m

3) From $438 to $443

4) From 256 ft to 140 ft

5) From 6469 ft to 7488 ft

6) From 36 inches to 90 inches

7) From 54 ft to 104 ft

8) From 84 miles to 24 miles

9) The population of a place in a particular year increased by 15%. Next year it decreased by 15%. Find the net increase or decrease percent in the initial population.

10) The salary of a doctor is increased by 40%. By what percent should the new salary be reduced in order to restore the original salary?

Markup, Discount, and Tax

Helpful Hints

- **Markup** = selling price − cost
  Markup rate = markup divided by the cost

- **Discount:**
  Multiply the regular price by the rate of discount

  Selling price =

  original price − discount

- **Tax:**
  To find tax, multiply the tax rate to the taxable amount (income, property value, etc.)

Example:

Original price of a microphone: $49.99, discount: 5%, tax: 5%

Selling price = 49.87

✎ *Find the selling price of each item.*

1) Cost of a pen: $1.95, markup: 70%, discount: 40%, tax: 5%

2) Cost of a puppy: $349.99, markup: 41%, discount: 23%

3) Cost of a shirt: $14.95, markup: 25%, discount: 45%

4) Cost of an oil change: $21.95, markup: 95%

5) Cost of computer: $1,850.00, markup: 75%

Test Preparation

1) Emma purchased a computer for $530.40. The computer is regularly priced at $624. What was the percent discount Emma received on the computer?

   A. 12%

   B. 15%

   C. 20%

   D. 25%

2) 125 students took an exam and 25 of them failed. What percent of the students passed the exam?

   A. 20 %
   B. 40 %
   C. 60 %
   D. 80 %

3) If 40 % of a class are girls, and 25 % of girls play tennis, what percent of the class play tennis?

   A. 10 %
   B. 15%
   C. 20 %
   D. 40 %

4) 1.2 is what percent of 24?

   A. 1.2

   B. 5

   C. 12

   D. 24

5) From last year, the price of gasoline has increased from $1.25 per gallon to $1.75 per gallon. The new price is what percent of the original price?

   A. 72 %

   B. 120 %

   C. 140 %

   D. 160 %

Answers of Worksheets – Chapter 4

Percentage Calculations

1) 12.5
2) 12
3) 10.2
4) 31.5
5) 0
6) 17.6
7) 5.2
8) 42.12
9) 40
10) 2
11) 16
12) 0
13) 14
14) 33
15) 8
16) 176
17) 70
18) 72
19) 67%
20) 70%
21) 58%
22) 50%

Converting Between Percent, Fractions, and Decimals

1) 0.5
2) 0.38
3) 0.15
4) 0.8
5) 0.07
6) 0.35
7) 0.9
8) 0.2
9) 0.07
10) 50%
11) 90%
12) 0.2%
13) 52.4%
14) 10%
15) 3%
16) 363%
17) 0.8%
18) 478%

Percent Problems

1) 15
2) 104.3
3) 38.34
4) 23.44%
5) 47.6%
6) 100
7) 515.4
8) 31.98
9) 1.9%
10) 8.3 m
11) 117 inches
12) 45.7 inches
13) 49 hours
14) 62.7%
15) Mathematics
16) 600

Find What Percentage a Number Is of Another

1) 45 is what percent of 90? 50 %
2) 15 is what percent of 75? 20 %
3) 20 is what percent of 400? 5 %
4) 18 is what percent of 90? 20 %
5) 3 is what percent of 15? 20 %
6) 8 is what percent of 80? 10 %
7) 11 is what percent of 55? 20 %
8) 9 is what percent of 90? 10 %
9) 2.5 is what percent of 10? 25 %
10) 5 is what percent of 25? 20 %
11) 60 is what percent of 20? 300 %
12) 12 is what percent of 48? 25 %
13) 14 is what percent of 28? 50 %
14) 8.2 is what percent of 32.8? 25 %
15) 1200 is what percent of 4,800? 25 %
16) 4,000 is what percent of 20,000? 20 %
17) 45 is what percent of 900? 5 %
18) 10 is what percent of 200? 5 %
19) 15 is what percent of 60? 25 %
20) 1.2 is what percent of 24? 5 %

Find a Percentage of a Given Number

1) 45
2) 20
3) 0
4) 64
5) 24
6) 30
7) 6
8) 3.5
9) 8
10) 6
11) 50
12) 30.6
13) 33.6
14) 10.8
15) 11.2
16) 16
17) 2.4
18) 26.6
19) 0.9
20) 20
21) 8

Percent of Increase and Decrease

1) 156.25% increase
2) 70% decrease
3) 1.142% increase
4) 45.31% decrease
5) 15.75% increase
6) 150% increase

7) 92.6% increase

8) 71.43% decrease

9) 2.25% decrease

10) $28\frac{4}{7}\%$

Markup, Discount, and Tax

1) $2.09
2) $379.98
3) $10.28
4) $36.22
5) $3,237.50

Test Preparation Answers

1) Choice B is correct

The question is this: 530.40 is what percent of 624?

Use percent formula:

$$\text{part} = \frac{\text{percent}}{100} \times \text{whole}$$

$530.40 = \frac{\text{percent}}{100} \times 624 \Rightarrow 530.40 = \frac{\text{percent} \times 624}{100} \Rightarrow 53040 = \text{percent} \times 624 \Rightarrow$

$\text{percent} = \frac{53040}{624} = 85$

530.40 is 85 % of 624. Therefore, the discount is: 100% − 85% = 15%

2) Choice D is correct.

The failing rate is 25 out of 125 = $\frac{25}{125}$

Change the fraction to percent:

$\frac{25}{125} \times 100\% = 20\%$

20 percent of students failed. Therefore, 80 percent of students passed the exam.

3) Choice A is correct

The percent of girls playing tennis is: 40 % × 25 % = 0.40 × 0.25 = 0.10 = 10 %

4) Choice B is correct.

x % of 24 is 1.2, then:

$\frac{x}{100} \times 24 = 1.2 \rightarrow \frac{24x}{100} = 1.2 \Rightarrow 24x = 1.2 \times 100 = 120 \rightarrow x = \frac{120}{24} = 5$

5) Choice C is correct

The question is this: 1.75 is what percent of 1.25?

Use percent formula:

$\text{part} = \frac{\text{percent}}{100} \times \text{whole}$

$\text{part} = \frac{\text{percent}}{100} \times 1.25 \Rightarrow 1.75 = \frac{\text{percent} \times 1.25}{100} \Rightarrow 175 = \text{percent} \times 1.25 \Rightarrow \text{percent} = \frac{175}{1.25} = 140$

Chapter 5: Algebraic Expressions

Topics that you'll learn in this chapter:

- ✓ Expressions and Variables
- ✓ Simplifying Variable Expressions
- ✓ Simplifying Polynomial Expressions
- ✓ Translate Phrases into an Algebraic Statement
- ✓ The Distributive Property
- ✓ Evaluating One Variable
- ✓ Evaluating Two Variables
- ✓ Combining like Terms

Expressions and Variables

Helpful Hints

A variable is a letter that represents unknown numbers. A variable can be used in the same manner as all other numbers:

Addition	2 + a	2 plus a
Subtraction	y – 3	y minus 3
Division	$\frac{4}{x}$	4 divided by x
Multiplication	5a	5 times a

✎ Simplify each expression.

1) $x + 5x$,
   use $x = 5$

2) $8(-3x + 9) + 6$,
   use $x = 6$

3) $10x - 2x + 6 - 5$,
   use $x = 5$

4) $2x - 3x - 9$,
   use $x = 7$

5) $(-6)(-2x - 4y)$,
   use $x = 1, y = 3$

6) $8x + 2 + 4y$,
   use $x = 9, y = 2$

7) $(-6)(-8x - 9y)$,
   use $x = 5, y = 5$

8) $6x + 5y$,
   use $x = 7, y = 4$

✎ Simplify each expression.

9) $5(-4 + 2x)$

10) $-3 - 5x - 6x + 9$

11) $6x - 3x - 8 + 10$

12) $(-8)(6x - 4) + 12$

13) $9(7x + 4) + 6x$

14) $(-9)(-5x + 2)$

Simplifying Variable Expressions

Helpful Hints
- Combine "like" terms. (values with same variable and same power)
- Use distributive property if necessary.

Distributive Property:
$a(b+c) = ab + ac$

Example:
$2x + 2(1-5x) =$

$2x + 2 - 10x = -8x + 2$

✎ Simplify each expression.

1) $-2 - x^2 - 6x^2$

2) $3 + 10x^2 + 2$

3) $8x^2 + 6x + 7x^2$

4) $5x^2 - 12x^2 + 8x$

5) $2x^2 - 2x - x$

6) $(-6)(8x - 4)$

7) $4x + 6(2 - 5x)$

8) $10x + 8(10x - 6)$

9) $9(-2x - 6) - 5$

10) $3(x + 9)$

11) $7x + 3 - 3x$

12) $2.5x^2 \times (-8x)$

✎ Simplify.

13) $-2(4 - 6x) - 3x$, $x = 1$

14) $2x + 8x$, $x = 2$

15) $9 - 2x + 5x + 2$, $x = 5$

16) $5(3x + 7)$, $x = 3$

17) $2(3 - 2x) - 4$, $x = 6$

18) $5x + 3x - 8$, $x = 3$

19) $x - 7x$, $x = 8$

20) $5(-2 - 9x)$, $x = 4$

Simplifying Polynomial Expressions

Helpful Hints

In mathematics, a polynomial is an expression consisting of variables and coefficients that involves only the operations of addition, subtraction, multiplication, and non–negative integer exponents of variables.

$P(x) = a_0 x^n + a_1 x^{n-1} + \ldots + a_{n-2} 2x^2 + a_{n-1} x + a_n$

Example:

An example of a polynomial of a single indeterminate x is

$x^2 - 4x + 7$.

An example for three variables is

$x^3 + 2xyz^2 - yz + 1$

✎ Simplify each polynomial.

1) $4x^5 - 5x^6 + 15x^5 - 12x^6 + 3x^6$

2) $(-3x^5 + 12 - 4x) + (8x^4 + 5x + 5x^5)$

3) $10x^2 - 5x^4 + 14x^3 - 20x^4 + 15x^3 - 8x^4$

4) $-6x^2 + 5x^2 - 7x^3 + 12 + 22$

5) $12x^5 - 5x^3 + 8x^2 - 8x^5$

6) $5x^3 + 1 + x^2 - 2x - 10x$

7) $14x^2 - 6x^3 - 2x(4x^2 + 2x)$

8) $(4x^4 - 2x) - (4x - 2x^4)$

9) $(3x^2 + 1) - (4 + 2x^2)$

10) $(2x + 2) - (7x + 6)$

11) $(12x^3 + 4x^4) - (2x^4 - 6x^3)$

12) $(12 + 3x^3) + (6x^3 + 6)$

13) $(5x^2 - 3) + (2x^2 - 3x^3)$

14) $(23x^3 - 12x^2) - (2x^2 - 9x^3)$

15) $(4x - 3x^3) - (3x^3 + 4x)$

Translate Phrases into an Algebraic Statement

> **Helpful Hints**
>
> Translating key words and phrases into algebraic expressions:
>
> **Addition:** plus, more than, the sum of, etc.
>
> **Subtraction:** minus, less than, decreased, etc.
>
> **Multiplication:** times, product, multiplied, etc.
>
> **Division:** quotient, divided, ratio, etc.
>
> **Example:**
>
> eight more than a number is 20
>
> $8 + x = 20$

✎ *Write an algebraic expression for each phrase.*

1) A number increased by forty–two.

2) The sum of fifteen and a number

3) The difference between fifty–six and a number.

4) The quotient of thirty and a number.

5) Twice a number decreased by 25.

6) Four times the sum of a number and − 12.

7) A number divided by − 20.

8) The quotient of 60 and the product of a number and − 5.

9) Ten subtracted from a number.

10) The difference of six and a number.

The Distributive Property

Helpful Hints

Distributive Property:

$a(b + c) = ab + ac$

Example:

$3(4 + 3x)$

$= 12 + 9x$

✎ Use the distributive property to simply each expression.

1) $-(-2 - 5x)$

2) $(-6x + 2)(-1)$

3) $(-5)(x - 2)$

4) $-(7 - 3x)$

5) $8(8 + 2x)$

6) $2(12 + 2x)$

7) $(-6x + 8)4$

8) $(3 - 6x)(-7)$

9) $(-12)(2x + 1)$

10) $(8 - 2x)9$

11) $(-2x)(-1 + 9x) - 4x(4 + 5x)$

12) $3(-5x - 3) + 4(6 - 3x)$

13) $(-2)(x + 4) - (2 + 3x)$

14) $(-4)(3x - 2) + 6(x + 1)$

15) $(-5)(4x - 1) + 4(x + 2)$

16) $(-3)(x + 4) - (2 + 3x)$

Evaluating One Variable

Helpful Hints

– To evaluate one variable expression, find the variable and substitute a number for that variable.

– Perform the arithmetic operations.

Example:

$4x + 8, x = 6$

$4(6) + 8 = 24 + 8 = 32$

✎ *Simplify each algebraic expression.*

1) $9 - x$, $x = 3$

2) $x + 2$, $x = 5$

3) $3x + 7$, $x = 6$

4) $x + (-5)$, $x = -2$

5) $3x + 6$, $x = 4$

6) $4x + 6$, $x = -1$

7) $10 + 2x - 6$, $x = 3$

8) $10 - 3x$, $x = 8$

9) $\frac{20}{x} - 3$, $x = 5$

10) $(-3) + \frac{x}{4} + 2x$, $x = 16$

11) $(-2) + \frac{x}{7}$, $x = 21$

12) $(-\frac{14}{x}) - 9 + 4x$, $x = 2$

13) $(-\frac{6}{x}) - 9 + 2x$, $x = 3$

14) $(-2) + \frac{x}{8}$, $x = 16$

15) $8(5x - 12)$, $x = -2$

Evaluating Two Variables

Helpful Hints

To evaluate an algebraic expression, substitute a number for each variable and perform the arithmetic operations.

Example:

$2x + 4y - 3 + 2,$

$x = 5, y = 3$

$2(5) + 4(3) - 3 + 2$
$= 10 + 12 - 3 + 2$
$= 21$

✎ *Simplify each algebraic expression.*

1) $2x + 4y - 3 + 2,$
   $x = 5, y = 3$

2) $(-\frac{12}{x}) + 1 + 5y,$
   $x = 6, y = 8$

3) $(-4)(-2a - 2b),$
   $a = 5, b = 3$

4) $10 + 3x + 7 - 2y,$
   $x = 7, y = 6$

5) $9x + 2 - 4y,$
   $x = 7, y = 5$

6) $6 + 3(-2x - 3y),$
   $x = 9, y = 7$

7) $12x + y,$
   $x = 4, y = 8$

8) $x \times 4 \div y,$
   $x = 3, y = 2$

9) $2x + 14 + 4y,$
   $x = 6, y = 8$

10) $4a - (5 - b),$
    $a = 4, b = 6$

Combining like Terms

Helpful Hints
- Terms are separated by "+" and "−" signs.
- Like terms are terms with same variables and same powers.
- Be sure to use the "+" or "−" that is in front of the coefficient.

Example:

$22x + 6 + 2x =$

$24x + 6$

✎ Simplify each expression.

1) $5 + 2x - 8$

2) $(-2x + 6)\,2$

3) $7 + 3x + 6x - 4$

4) $(-4) - (3)(5x + 8)$

5) $9x - 7x - 5$

6) $x - 12x$

7) $7\,(3x + 6) + 2x$

8) $(-11x) - 10x$

9) $3x - 12 - 5x$

10) $13 + 4x - 5$

11) $(-22x) + 8x$

12) $2\,(4 + 3x) - 7x$

13) $(-4x) - (6 - 14x)$

14) $5\,(6x - 1) + 12x$

15) $22x + 6 + 2x$

16) $(-13x) - 14x$

17) $(-6x) - 9 + 15x$

18) $(-6x) + 7x$

19) $(-5x) + 12 + 7x$

20) $(-3x) - 9 + 15x$

21) $20x - 19x$

Test Preparation

1) If $x = -8$, which equation is true?

   A. $x(2x - 4) = 120$

   B. $8(4 - x) = 96$

   C. $2(4x + 6) = 79$

   D. $6x + 2 = -50$

2) Which of the following points lies on the line $4x + 6y = 14$?

   A. (2, 1)

   B. (−1, 3)

   C. (−3, 4)

   D. (2, 2)

3) Mike is 7.5 miles ahead of Julia running at 5.5 miles per hour and Julia is running at the speed of 6 miles per hour. How long does it take Julia to catch Mike?

   A. 2 hours
   B. 5.5 hours
   C. 7.5 hours
   D. 15 hours

4) Which of the following points lies on the line $2x + 4y = 10$

   A. (2, 1)
   B. (−1, 3)
   C. (−2, 2)
   D. (2, 2)

5) A company pays its employer $7,000 plus 2% of all sales profit. If x is the number of all sales profit, which of the following represents the employer's revenue?

   A. $0.02x$
   B. $0.98x - 7,000$
   C. $0.02x + 7,000$
   D. $0.98x + 7,000$

Answers of Worksheets – Chapter 5

Expressions and Variables

1) 30
2) −66
3) 41
4) −16
5) 84
6) 82
7) 510
8) 62
9) $10x − 20$
10) $6 − 11x$
11) $3x + 2$
12) $44 − 48x$
13) $69x + 36$
14) $45x − 18$

Simplifying Variable Expressions

1) $−7x^2 − 2$
2) $10x^2 + 5$
3) $15x^2 + 6x$
4) $−7x^2 + 8x$
5) $2x^2 − 3x$
6) $−48x + 24$
7) $−26x + 12$
8) $90x − 48$
9) $−18x − 59$
10) $3x + 27$
11) $4x + 3$
12) $−20x^3$
13) 1
14) 20
15) 26
16) 80
17) −22
18) 16
19) −48
20) −190

Simplifying Polynomial Expressions

1) $−14x^6 + 19x^5$
2) $2x^5 + 8x^4 + x + 12$
3) $−33x^4 + 29x^3 + 10x^2$
4) $−7x^3 − x^2 + 34$
5) $4x^5 − 5x^3 + 8x^2$
6) $5x^3 + x^2 − 12x + 1$
7) $−14x^3 + 10x^2$
8) $6x^4 − 6x$
9) $x^2 − 3$
10) $−5x − 4$
11) $2x^4 + 18x^3$
12) $9x^3 + 18$
13) $−3x^3 + 7x^2 − 3$
14) $32x^3 − 14x^2$
15) $−6x^3$

Translate Phrases into an Algebraic Statement

1) $x + 42$
2) $15 + x$
3) $56 − x$
4) $30/x$
5) $2x − 25$
6) $4(x + (−12))$
7) $\dfrac{x}{-20}$
8) $\dfrac{60}{-5x}$
9) $x − 10$
10) $6 − x$

The Distributive Property

1) 5x + 2
2) 6x − 2
3) −5x + 10
4) 3x − 7
5) 16x + 64
6) 4x + 24
7) − 24x + 32
8) 42x − 21
9) − 24x − 12
10) − 18x + 72
11) − 38x^2 − 14x
12) − 27x + 15
13) − 5x − 10
14) − 6x + 14
15) − 16x + 13
16) − 6x − 14

Evaluating One Variable

1) 6
2) 7
3) 25
4) −7
5) 18
6) 2
7) 10
8) −14
9) 1
10) 33
11) 1
12) −8
13) −5
14) 0
15) −176

Evaluating Two Variables

1) 21
2) 39
3) 64
4) 26
5) 45
6) −111
7) 56
8) 6
9) 58
10) 17

Combining like Terms

1) 2x − 3
2) −4x + 12
3) 9x + 3
4) −15x − 28
5) 2x − 5
6) −11x
7) 23x + 42
8) −21x
9) −2x − 12
10) 4x + 8
11) −14x
12) − x + 8
13) 10x − 6
14) 42x − 5
15) 24x + 6
16) −27x
17) 9x − 9
18) x
19) 2x + 12
20) 12x − 9
21) x

Test Preparation Answers

1) Choice B is correct.

$x = -8$, then:

  A. $(-8)(2(-8) - 4) = 120 \rightarrow 160 = 120$ Wrong!
  B. $8(4 - (-8)) = 96 \rightarrow 96 = 96$ Correct!
  C. $2(4(-8) + 6) = 79 \rightarrow -52 = 79$ Wrong!
  D. $6(-8) + 2 = -50 \rightarrow -46 = -50$ Wrong!

2) Choice A is correct.

Plug in each pair of numbers in the equation. The answer should be 14.

  A. (2, 1):   4 (2) + 6 (1) = 14   Yes!
  B. (−1, 3):   4 (−1) + 6 (2) = 8   No!
  C. (−2, 2):   4 (−2) + 6 (2) = 4   No!
  D. (2, 2):   4 (2) + 6 (2) = 20   No!

3) Choice D is correct.

The distance that Mike runs can be found by the following equation:

$D_M = 5.5t + 7.5$

The distance Julia runs can be found by $D_J = 6t$

Julia catches Mike if they run the same distance. Therefore,

$6t = 5.5t + 7.5$

$0.5t = 7.5 \rightarrow t = \dfrac{7.5}{0.5} = 15 \: hours$

4) Choice B is correct.

Plug in each pair of numbers in the equation. The answer should be 10

    A. (2, 1):   2 (2) + 4 (1) = 8
    B. (−1, 3):   2 (−1) + 4 (3) = 10
    C. (−2, 2):   2 (−2) + 4 (2) = 4
    D. (2, 2):   2 (2) + 4 (2) = 12

5) Choice C is correct

x is the number of all sales profit and 2% of it is:

$$2\% \times x = 0.02x$$

Employer's revenue: $0.2x + 7000$

Chapter 6: Equations

Topics that you'll learn in this chapter:

- ✓ One–Step Equations
- ✓ One–Step Equation Word Problems
- ✓ Two–Step Equations
- ✓ Two–Step Equation Word Problems
- ✓ Multi–Step Equations

One–Step Equations

Helpful Hints
- The values of two expressions on both sides of an equation are equal.
$$ax + b = c$$
- You only need to perform one Math operation in order to solve the equation.

Example:

$-8x = 16$

$x = -2$

✏️ **Solve each equation.**

1) x + 3 = 17

2) 22 = (− 8) + x

3) 3x = (− 30)

4) (− 36) = (− 6x)

5) (− 6) = 4 + x

6) 2 + x = (− 2)

7) 20x = (− 220)

8) 18 = x + 5

9) (− 23) + x = (− 19)

10) 5x = (− 45)

11) x − 12 = (− 25)

12) x − 3 = (− 12)

13) (− 35) = x − 27

14) 8 = 2x

15) (− 6x) = 36

16) (− 55) = (− 5x)

17) x − 30 = 20

18) 8x = 32

19) 36 = (− 4x)

20) 4x = 68

21) 30x = 300

One–Step Equation Word Problems

> **Helpful Hints**
> – Define the variable.
> – Translate key words and phrases into math equation.
> – Isolate the variable and solve the equation.

✎ Solve.

1) How many boxes of envelopes can you buy with $18 if one box costs $3?

2) After paying $6.25 for a salad, Ella has $45.56. How much money did she have before buying the salad?

3) How many packages of diapers can you buy with $50 if one package costs $5?

4) Last week James ran 20 miles more than Michael. James ran 56 miles. How many miles did Michael run?

5) Last Friday Jacob had $32.52. Over the weekend he received some money for cleaning the attic. He now has $44. How much money did he receive?

6) After paying $10.12 for a sandwich, Amelia has $35.50. How much money did she have before buying the sandwich?

Two–Step Equations

Helpful Hints
- You only need to perform two math operations (add, subtract, multiply, or divide) to solve the equation.
- Simplify using the inverse of addition or subtraction.
- Simplify further by using the inverse of multiplication or division.

Example:

$-2(x-1) = 42$

$(x-1) = -21$

$x = -20$

✍ Solve each equation.

1) $5(8+x) = 20$

2) $(-7)(x-9) = 42$

3) $(-12)(2x-3) = (-12)$

4) $6(1+x) = 12$

5) $12(2x+4) = 60$

6) $7(3x+2) = 42$

7) $8(14+2x) = (-34)$

8) $(-15)(2x-4) = 48$

9) $3(x+5) = 12$

10) $\dfrac{3x-12}{6} = 4$

11) $(-12) = \dfrac{x+15}{6}$

12) $110 = (-5)(2x-6)$

13) $\dfrac{x}{8} - 12 = 4$

14) $20 = 12 + \dfrac{x}{4}$

15) $\dfrac{-24+x}{6} = (-12)$

16) $(-4)(5+2x) = (-100)$

17) $(-12x) + 20 = 32$

18) $\dfrac{-2+6x}{4} = (-8)$

19) $\dfrac{x+6}{5} = (-5)$

20) $(-9) + \dfrac{x}{4} = (-15)$

Two–Step Equation Word Problems

> **Helpful Hints**
> – Translate the word problem into equations with variables.
> – Solve the equations to find the solutions to the word problems.

✏️ Solve.

1) The sum of three consecutive even numbers is 48. What is the smallest of these numbers?

2) How old am I if 400 reduced by 2 times my age is 244?

3) For a field trip, 4 students rode in cars and the rest filled nine buses. How many students were in each bus if 472 students were on the trip?

4) The sum of three consecutive numbers is 72. What is the smallest of these numbers?

5) 331 students went on a field trip. Six buses were filled, and 7 students traveled in cars. How many students were in each bus?

6) You bought a magazine for $5 and four erasers. You spent a total of $25. How much did each eraser cost?

Multi–Step Equations

Helpful Hints

– Combine "like" terms on one side.

– Bring variables to one side by adding or subtracting.

– Simplify using the inverse of addition or subtraction.

– Simplify further by using the inverse of multiplication or division.

Example:

$3x + 15 = -2x + 5$

Add 2x both sides

$5x + 15 = +5$

Subtract 15 both sides

$5x = -10$

Divide by 5 both sides

$x = -2$

✎ Solve each equation.

1) $-(2 - 2x) = 10$

2) $-12 = -(2x + 8)$

3) $3x + 15 = (-2x) + 5$

4) $-28 = (-2x) - 12x$

5) $2(1 + 2x) + 2x = -118$

6) $3x - 18 = 22 + x - 3 + x$

7) $12 - 2x = (-32) - x + x$

8) $7 - 3x - 3x = 3 - 3x$

9) $6 + 10x + 3x = (-30) + 4x$

10) $(-3x) - 8(-1 + 5x) = 352$

11) $24 = (-4x) - 8 + 8$

12) $9 = 2x - 7 + 6x$

13) $6(1 + 6x) = 294$

14) $-10 = (-4x) - 6x$

15) $4x - 2 = (-7) + 5x$

16) $5x - 14 = 8x + 4$

17) $40 = -(4x - 8)$

18) $(-18) - 6x = 6(1 + 3x)$

19) $x - 5 = -2(6 + 3x)$

20) $6 = 1 - 2x + 5$

Test Preparation

1) Jason needs an 75% average in his writing class to pass. On his first 4 exams, he earned scores of 68%, 72%, 85%, and 90%. What is the minimum score Jason can earn on his fifth and final test to pass?

   Write your answer in the box below.

   ☐

2) Which set of ordered pairs represents y as a function of x?

   A. $\{(1, -5), (12, 4), (5, -2), (1, -7)\}$

   B. $\{(2, 2), (5, -9), (5, 8), (8, 4)\}$

   C. $\{(2, -6), (1, 12), (5, 10), (-2, 1)\}$

   D. $\{(7, 11), (6, 5), (7, 5), (3, -5)\}$

3) An angle is equal to one fifth of its supplement. What is the measure of that angle?

   A. 20

   B. 30

   C. 45

   D. 60

4) Which graph shows a non–proportional linear relationship between x and y?

A.

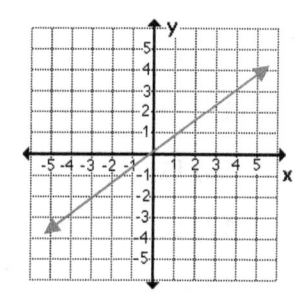

B.

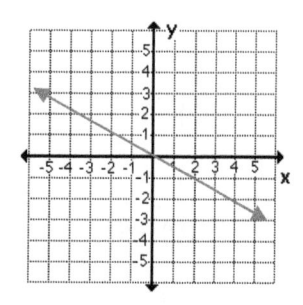

C.

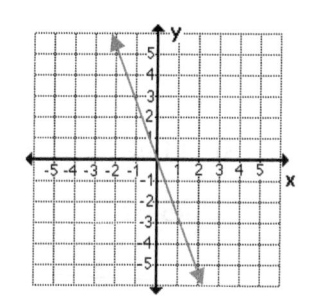

D.

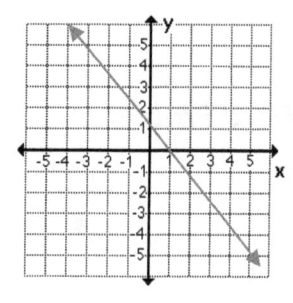

5) Which set of ordered pairs represents y as a function of x?

A. {(3, −2), (3, 7), (9, −8), (4, −7)}

B. {(4, 2), (3, −9), (5, 8), (4, 7)}

C. {(9, 12), (5, 7), (6, 11), (5, 18)}

D. {(6, 1), (3, 1), (0, 5), (4, 5)}

Answers of Worksheets – Chapter 6

One–Step Equations

1) 14
2) 30
3) − 10
4) 6
5) − 10
6) − 4
7) − 11
8) 13
9) 4
10) − 9
11) − 13
12) − 9
13) − 8
14) 4
15) − 6
16) 11
17) 50
18) 4
19) − 9
20) 17
21) 10

One–Step Equation Word Problems

1) 6
2) $51.81
3) 10
4) 36
5) 11.48
6) 45.62

Two–Step Equations

1) − 4
2) 3
3) 2
4) 1
5) 0.5
6) $\frac{4}{3}$
7) $-\frac{73}{8}$
8) $\frac{2}{5}$
9) − 1
10) 12
11) − 87
12) − 8
13) 128
14) 32
15) − 48
16) 10
17) − 1
18) − 5
19) − 31
20) − 24

Two–Step Equation Word Problems

1) 14
2) 78
3) 52
4) 23
5) 54
6) $4

Multi–Step Equations

1) 6
2) 2
3) −2
4) 2
5) −20
6) 37
7) 22
8) $\frac{4}{3}$
9) −4
10) −8
11) −6
12) 2
13) 8
14) 1
15) 5
16) −6
17) −8
18) −1
19) −1
20) 0

Test Preparation Answers

1) The answer is 60.

Jason needs an 75% average to pass the exams. Therefore, the sum of 5 exams must be at least 5 × 75 = 375

The sum of 4 exams is:

68 + 72 + 85 + 90 = 315.

The minimum score Jason can earn on his fifth and final test to pass is:

375 − 315 = 60

2) Choice C is correct.

A set of ordered pairs represents y as a function of x if:

$x_1 = x_2 \rightarrow y_1 = y_2$

In choice A: (1, -5) and (1, -7) are ordered pairs with same x and different y, therefore y isn't a function of x.

In choice B: (5, -9) and (5, 8) are ordered pairs with same x and different y, therefore y isn't a function of x.

In choice D: (7, 11) and (7, 5) are ordered pairs with same x and different y, therefore y isn't a function of x.

3) Choice B is correct.

Let x be the amount of angle and y be the amount of its supplement. The angle and its supplement are 180° in total ($x + y = 180°$). we have: $x = \frac{1}{5} y$

$x + y = \frac{1}{5} y + y = 180° \Rightarrow y = 150°$ and $x = 30°$

4) Choice D is correct.

A linear equation is a relationship between two variables, x and y, and can be written in the form of $y = mx + b$.

A non-proportional linear relationship takes on the form $y = mx + b$, where $b \neq 0$ and its graph is a line that does not cross through the origin.

5) Choice D is correct.

A set of ordered pairs represents y as a function of x if:

$$x_1 = x_2 \rightarrow y_1 = y_2$$

In choice A: (3, -2) and (3, 7) are ordered pairs with same x and different y, therefore y isn't a function of x.

In choice B: (4, 2) and (4, 7) are ordered pairs with same x and different y, therefore y isn't a function of x.

In choice C: (5, 7) and (5, 18) are ordered pairs with same x and different y, therefore y isn't a function of x.

Chapter 7: Systems of Equations

Topics that you'll learn in this chapter:

- ✓ Solving Systems of Equations by Substitution
- ✓ Solving Systems of Equations by Elimination
- ✓ Systems of Equations Word Problems

Solving Systems of Equations by Substitution

> **Helpful Hints**
>
> Consider the system of equations
> $x - y = 1, -2x + y = 6$
> Substitute $x = 1 - y$ in the second equation
> $-2(1 - y) + y = 5 \quad y = 2$
> Substitute $y = 2$ in $x = 1 + y$
> $x = 1 + 2 = 3$
>
> **Example:**
> $-2x - 2y = -13$
> $-4x + 2y = 10$
>
> $(0.5, 6)$

Solve each system of equation by substitution.

1) $-2x + 2y = 4$
   $-2x + y = 3$

2) $-10x + 2y = -6$
   $6x - 16y = 48$

3) $y = -8$
   $16x - 12y = 72$

4) $2y = -6x + 10$
   $10x - 8y = -6$

5) $3x - 9y = -3$
   $3y = 3x - 3$

6) $-4x + 12y = 12$
   $-14x + 16y = -10$

Solving Systems of Equations by Elimination

Helpful Hints - The elimination method for solving systems of linear equations uses the addition property of equality. You can add the same value to each side of an equation.

Example:
$$x + 2y = 6$$
$$+ \; -x + y = 3$$
$$3y = 9$$
$$y = 3$$
$$x + 6 = 6$$
$$x = 0$$

Solve each system of equation by elimination.

1) $10x - 9y = -12$
   $-5x + 3y = 6$

2) $-3x - 4y = 5$
   $x - 2y = 5$

3) $5x - 14y = 22$
   $-6x + 7y = 3$

4) $10x - 14y = -4$
   $-10x - 20y = -30$

5) $32x + 14y = 52$
   $16x - 4y = -40$

6) $2x - 8y = -6$
   $8x + 2y = 10$

7) $-4x + 4y = -4$
   $4x + 2y = 10$

8) $4x + 6y = 10$
   $8x + 12y = -20$

Systems of Equations Word Problems

> **Helpful Hints**
> Define your variables, write two equations, and use one of the methods for solving systems of equations.

Example:

The difference of two numbers is 6. Their sum is 14. Find the numbers.

$x + y = 6$

$x + y = 14$ (10, 4)

1) A farmhouse shelters 10 animals, some are pigs and some are ducks. Altogether there are 36 legs. How many of each animal are there?

2) A class Of 195 students went on a field trip. They took vehicles, some cars and some buses. Find the number of cars and the number of buses they took if each car holds 5 students and each bus hold 45 students.

3) The sum of the digits of a certain two-digit number is 7. Reversing its increasing the number by 9. What is the number?

4) A boat traveled 336 miles downstream and back. The trip downstream took 12 hours. The trip back took 14 hours. What is the speed of the boat in still water? What is the speed of the current?

Test Preparation

1) What is the solution of the following system of equations?

$$\begin{cases} \dfrac{-x}{2} + \dfrac{y}{4} = 1 \\ \dfrac{-5y}{6} + 2x = 4 \end{cases}$$

A. $x = 48, y = 22$

B. $x = 50, y = 20$

C. $x = 20, y = 50$

D. $x = 22, y = 48$

2) Which of the following values for x and y satisfy the following system of equations?

$$\begin{cases} x + 4y = 10 \\ 5x + 10y = 20 \end{cases}$$

A. $x = 3, y = 2$

B. $x = 2, y - 3$

C. $x = -2, y = 3$

D. $x = 3, y = -2$

Answers of Worksheets – Chapter 7

Solving Systems of Equations by Substitution

1) (4, 9)
2) (−1, 1)
3) (0, −3)
4) (−24, −8)
5) (1, 2)
6) (4, 3)
7) (3, 2)
8) (−5, 1)

Solving Systems of Equations by Elimination

1) (15, 27)
2) (1, −2)
3) (−4, −3)
4) (1, 1)
5) (−1, 6)
6) (1, 1)
7) (2, 1)
8) No solution
9) (3, 4)
10) (4, 2)

Systems of Equations Word Problems

1) (2, 8)
2) (3, 4)
3) (10, 4)
4) 34
5) boat: 26 mph, current: 2 mph

Test Preparation Answers

1) Choice D is correct

$\begin{cases} \frac{-x}{2} + \frac{y}{4} = 1 \\ \frac{-5y}{6} + 2x = 4 \end{cases} \rightarrow$ Multiply the top equation by 4. Then,

$\begin{cases} -2x + y = 4 \\ \frac{-5y}{6} + 2x = 4 \end{cases} \rightarrow$ Add two equations.

$\frac{1}{6}y = 8 \rightarrow y = 48$, plug in the value of y into the first equation $\rightarrow x = 22$

2) Choice C is correct

$\begin{cases} x + 4y = 10 \\ 5x + 10y = 20 \end{cases} \rightarrow$ Multiply the top equation by -5 then,

$\begin{cases} -5x - 20y = -50 \\ 5x + 10y = 20 \end{cases} \rightarrow$ Add two equations

$-10y = -30 \rightarrow y = 3$, plug in the value of y into the first equation

$$x + 4y = 10 \rightarrow x + 4(3) = 10 \rightarrow x + 12 = 10$$

Subtract 12 from both sides of the equation. Then:

$$x + 12 = 10 \rightarrow x = -2$$

Chapter 8: Inequalities

Topics that you'll learn in this chapter:

- ✓ Graphing Single– Variable Inequalities
- ✓ One– Step Inequalities
- ✓ Two– Step Inequalities
- ✓ Multi– Step Inequalities

Graphing Single–Variable Inequalities

Helpful Hints

– Isolate the variable.

– Find the value of the inequality on the number line.

– For less than or greater than draw open circle on the value of the variable.

– If there is an equal sign too, then use filled circle.

– Draw a line to the right direction.

✎ *Draw a graph for each inequality.*

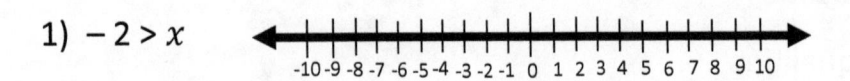

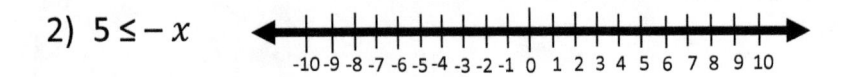

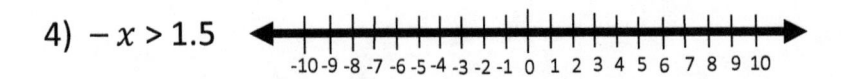

1) $-2 > x$ ←|||||||||||||||||||||→
                    -10 -9 -8 -7 -6 -5 -4 -3 -2 -1 0 1 2 3 4 5 6 7 8 9 10

2) $5 \leq -x$ ←|||||||||||||||||||||→
                    -10 -9 -8 -7 -6 -5 -4 -3 -2 -1 0 1 2 3 4 5 6 7 8 9 10

3) $x > 7$ ←|||||||||||||||||||||→
                    -10 -9 -8 -7 -6 -5 -4 -3 -2 -1 0 1 2 3 4 5 6 7 8 9 10

4) $-x > 1.5$ ←|||||||||||||||||||||→
                    -10 -9 -8 -7 -6 -5 -4 -3 -2 -1 0 1 2 3 4 5 6 7 8 9 10

One–Step Inequalities

Helpful Hints

— Isolate the variable.

— For dividing both sides by negative numbers, flip the direction of the inequality sign.

Example:

$x + 4 \geq 11$

$x \geq 7$

✎ *Solve each inequality and graph it.*

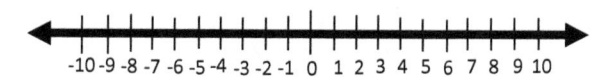

1) $x + 9 \geq 11$

2) $x - 4 \leq 2$

3) $6x \geq 36$

4) $7 + x < 16$

5) $x + 8 \leq 1$

6) $3x > 12$

7) $3x < 24$

Two–Step Inequalities

Helpful Hints

– Isolate the variable.

– For dividing both sides by negative numbers, flip the direction of the of the inequality sign.

– Simplify using the inverse of addition or subtraction.

– Simplify further by using the inverse of multiplication or division.

Example:

$2x + 9 \geq 11$

$2x \geq 2$

$x \geq 1$

✎Solve each inequality and graph it.

1) $3x - 4 \leq 5$

2) $2x - 2 \leq 6$

3) $4x - 4 \leq 8$

4) $3x + 6 \geq 12$

5) $6x - 5 \geq 19$

6) $2x - 4 \leq 6$

7) $8x - 4 \leq 4$

8) $6x + 4 \leq 10$

9) $5x + 4 \leq 9$

10) $7x - 4 \leq 3$

11) $4x - 19 < 19$

12) $2x - 3 < 21$

13) $7 + 4x \geq 19$

14) $9 + 4x < 21$

15) $3 + 2x \geq 19$

16) $6 + 4x < 22$

Multi–Step Inequalities

Helpful *Hints*	– Isolate the variable. – Simplify using the inverse of addition or subtraction. – Simplify further by using the inverse of multiplication or division.	Example: $\dfrac{7x+1}{3} \geq 5$ $7x + 1 \geq 15$ $7x \geq 14$ $x \geq 7$

✎Solve each inequality.

1) $\dfrac{9x}{7} - 7 < 2$

2) $\dfrac{4x + 8}{2} \leq 12$

3) $\dfrac{3x - 8}{7} > 1$

4) $-3(x - 7) > 21$

5) $4 + \dfrac{x}{3} < 7$

6) $\dfrac{2x + 6}{4} \leq 10$

www.EffortlessMath.com   117

Test Preparation

1) Which value of x makes the following inequality true?

$$\frac{3}{22} \leq x < 19\%$$

A. 0.13

B. $\frac{5}{36}$

C. $\sqrt{0.044}$

D. 0.124

2) Which of the following graphs represents the compound inequality $-2 \leq 2x - 4 < 8$?

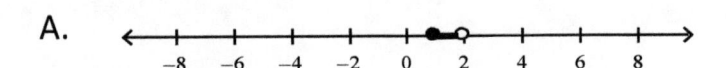

A.

B.

C.

D.

3) Which graph corresponds to the following inequalities?

$y \leq x+4$

$2x+y \leq -4$

A.

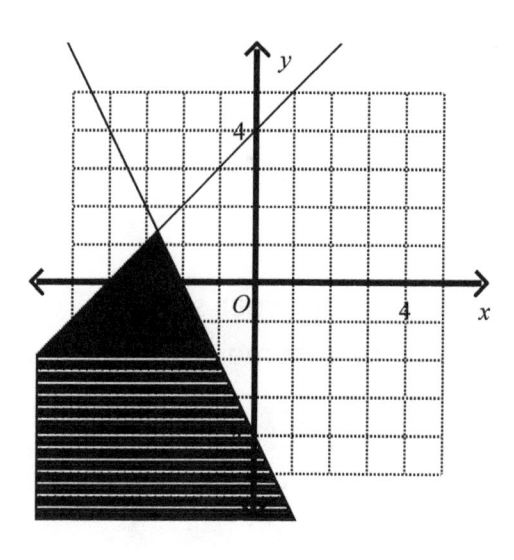

B.

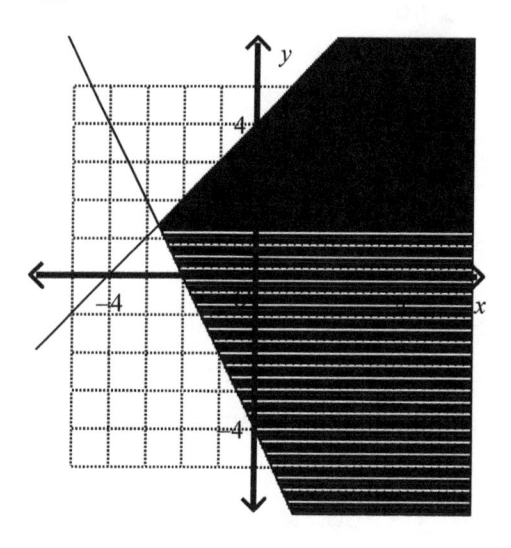

C.

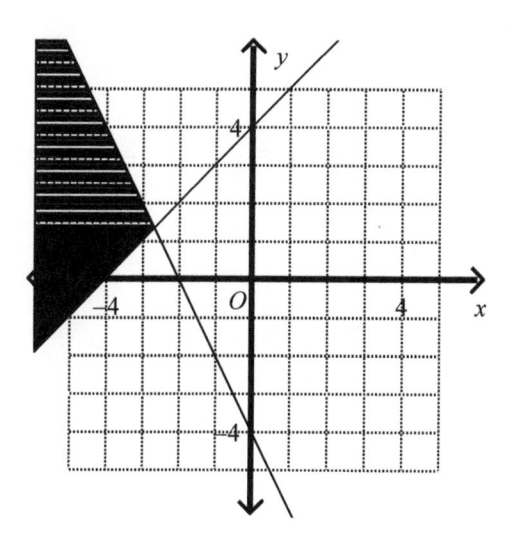

D.

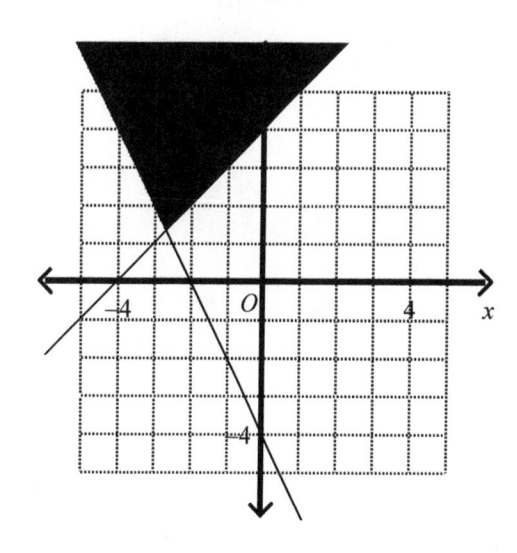

4) Which value of x makes the following inequality true?

$$\frac{2}{21} \leq x < 14\%$$

A. 0.013

B. $\frac{5}{66}$

C. $\sqrt{0.044}$

D. 0.124

5) In 1999, the average worker's income increased $2,000 per year starting from $24,000 annual salary. Which equation represents income greater than average? (I = income, x = number of years after 1999)

A. I > 2000 x + 24000

B. I > − 2000 x + 24000

C. I < −2000 x + 24000

D. I < 2000 x − 24000

Answers of Worksheets – Chapter 8

Graphing Single–Variable Inequalities

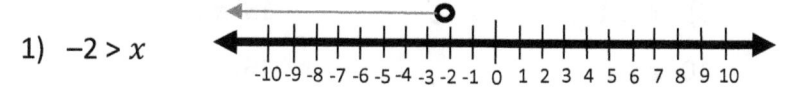

1) $-2 > x$

2) $x \leq -5$

3) $x > 7$

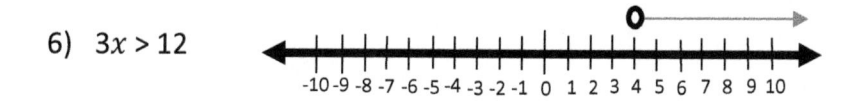

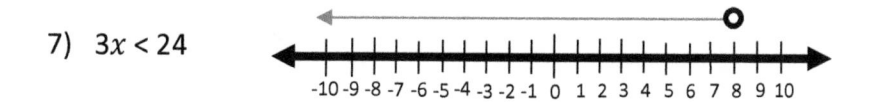

4) $-1.5 > x$

One–Step Inequalities

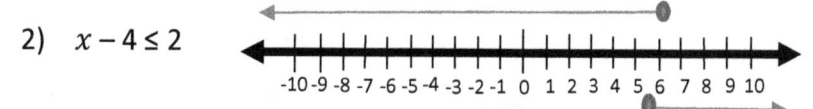

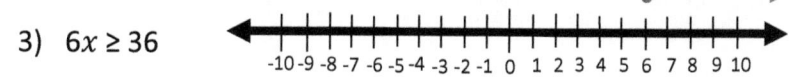

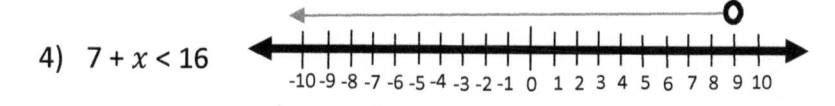

1) $x + 9 \geq 11$

2) $x - 4 \leq 2$

3) $6x \geq 36$

4) $7 + x < 16$

5) $x + 8 \leq 1$

6) $3x > 12$

7) $3x < 24$

Two–Step inequalities

1) $x \leq 3$
2) $x \leq 4$
3) $x \leq 3$
4) $x \geq 2$
5) $x \geq 4$
6) $x \leq 5$
7) $x \leq 1$
8) $x \leq 1$
9) $x \leq 1$
10) $x \leq 1$
11) $x < 9.5$
12) $x < 12$
13) $x \geq 3$
14) $x < 3$
15) $x \geq 8$
16) $x < 4$

Multi–Step inequalities

1) $x < 7$
2) $x \leq 4$
3) $x > 5$
4) $x < 0$
5) $x < 9$
6) $x \leq 17$

Test Preparation Answers

1) Choice B is correct.

$\frac{3}{22}$ = 0.136 and 19% = 0.19 therefore x should be between 0.136 and 0.19

Choice B. $\frac{5}{36}$ = 0.138 is between 0.136 and 0.19

2) Choice D is correct.

Solve for x.

$-2 \leq 2x - 4 < 8 \Rightarrow$ (add 4 all sides) $-2 + 4 \leq 2x - 4 + 4 < 8 + 4 \Rightarrow$

$2 \leq 2x < 12 \Rightarrow$ (divide all sides by 2) $1 \leq x < 6$

x is between 1 and 6.

3) Choice A is correct

For each option, choose a point in the solution part and check it on both inequalities.

$y \leq x + 4$

$2x + y \leq -4$

   A. Point (−4, −4) is in the solution section. Let's check the point in both inequalities.

−4 ≤ − 4 + 4, It works

2 (−4) + (−4) ≤ −4 ⇒ − 12 ≤ − 4, it works (this point works in both)

   B. Let's choose this point (0, 0)
      0 ≤ 0 + 4, It works
      2 (0) + (0) ≤ −4, That's not true!

   C. Let's choose this point (−5, 0)
      0 ≤ −5 + 4, That's not true!

   D. Let's choose this point (0, 5)
      5 ≤ 0 + 4, That's not true!

4) Choice D is correct.

x is between 0.09 and 0.14

Choice D is correct.

5) Choice A is correct

Let x be the number of years. Therefore, $2,000 per year equals $2000x$.

starting from $24,000 annual salary means you should add that amount to $2000x$.

Income more than that is:

I > 2000x + 24000

Chapter 9: Linear Functions

Topics that you'll learn in this chapter:

- ✓ Finding Slope
- ✓ Graphing Lines Using Slope–Intercept Form
- ✓ Graphing Lines Using Standard Form
- ✓ Writing Linear Equations
- ✓ Graphing Linear Inequalities
- ✓ Finding Midpoint
- ✓ Finding Distance of Two Points
- ✓ Slope and Rate of Change
- ✓ Find the Slope, X–intercept and Y–intercept
- ✓ Write an Equation from a Graph
- ✓ Slope–intercept form
- ✓ Point–slope form
- ✓ Equations of horizontal and vertical lines
- ✓ Equation of parallel or perpendicular lines

Finding Slope

Helpful Hints

Slope of a line:

$$\frac{y_2 - y_1}{x_2 - x_1} = \frac{rise}{run}$$

Example:

(2, −10), (3, 6)

slope = 16

✎ **Find the slope of the line through each pair of points.**

1) (1, 1), (3, 5)

2) (4, −6), (−3, −8)

3) (7, −12), (5, 10)

4) (19, 3), (20, 3)

5) (15, 8), (−17, 9)

6) (6, −12), (15, −3)

7) (3, 1), (7, −5)

8) (3, −2), (−7, 8)

9) (15, −3), (−9, 5)

10) (−4, 7), (−6, −4)

11) (6, −8), (−11, −7)

12) (−6, 13), (17, −9)

13) (−10, −2), (−6, −5)

14) (4, 5), (−4, 10)

15) (−3, 1), (−17, 2)

16) (7, 0), (−13, −11)

17) (17, −13), (17, 8)

18) (12, 2), (−7, 5)

Graphing Lines Using Slope–Intercept Form

> **Helpful Hints**
>
> **Slope–intercept form:** given the slope m and the y–intercept b, then the equation of the line is:
>
> $y = mx + b$.

Example:

$y = 8x - 3$

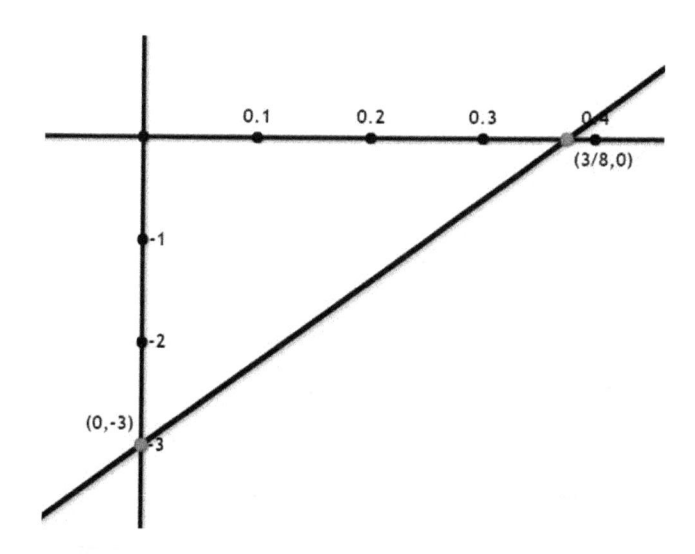

😊 **Sketch the graph of each line.**

1) $y = \dfrac{1}{2}x - 4$

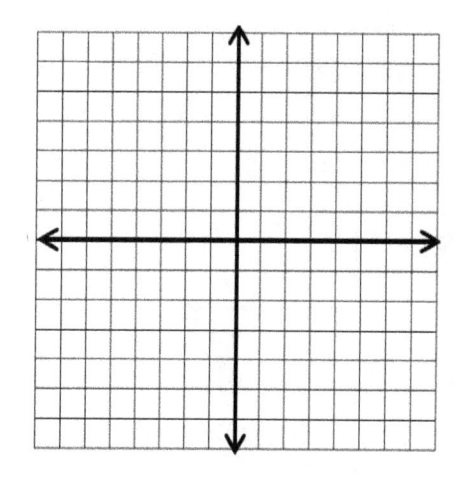

2) $y = 2x$

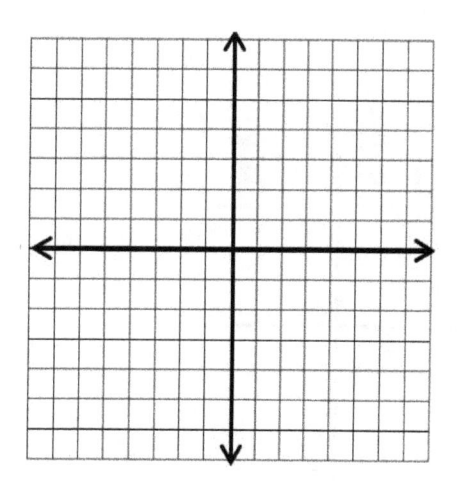

Graphing Lines Using Standard Form

Helpful Hints
- Find the –intercept of the line by putting zero for y.
- Find the y-intercept of the line by putting zero for the x.
- Connect these two points.

Example:

$x + 4y = 12$

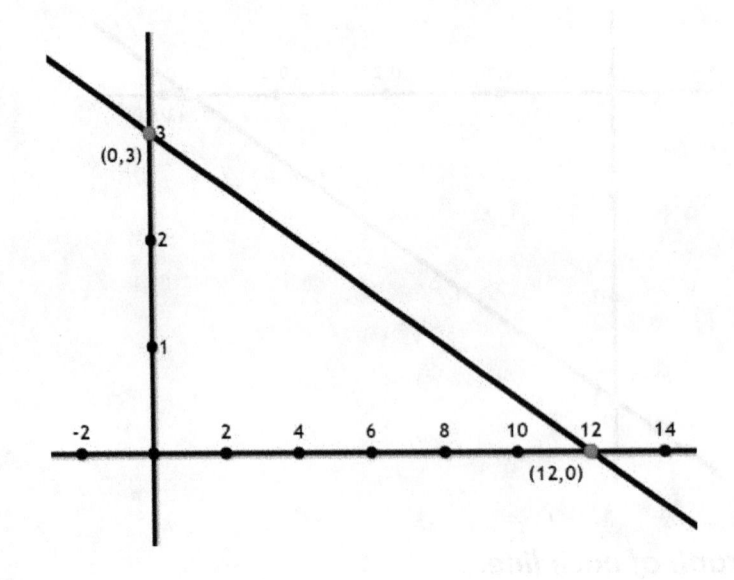

Sketch the graph of each line.

1) $2x - y = 4$

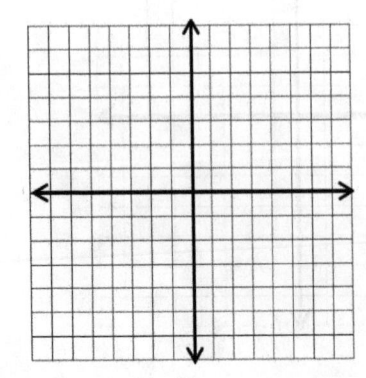

2) $x + y = 2$

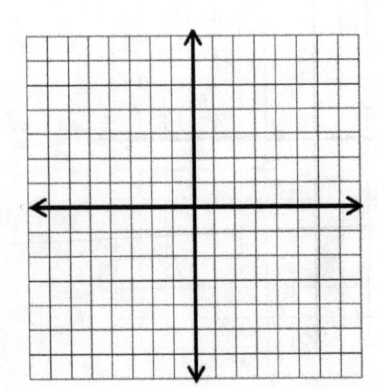

Writing Linear Equations

Helpful Hints

The equation of a line:

$$y = mx + b$$

1– Identify the slope.

2– Find the y–intercept. This can be done by substituting the slope and the coordinates of a point (x, y) on the line.

Example:

through:

$(-4, -2), (-3, 5)$

$y = 7x + 26$

✏ *Write the slope–intercept form of the equation of the line through the given points.*

1) through: $(-4, -2), (-3, 5)$

2) through: $(5, 4), (-4, 3)$

3) through: $(0, -2), (-5, 3)$

4) through: $(-1, 1), (-2, 6)$

5) through: $(0, 3), (-4, -1)$

6) through: $(0, 2), (1, -3)$

7) through: $(0, -5), (4, 3)$

8) through: $(-1, 4), (0, 4)$

9) through: $(2, -3), (3, -5)$

10) through: $(2, 5), (-1, -4)$

11) through: $(1, -3), (-3, 1)$

12) through: $(3, 3), (1, -5)$

13) through: $(4, 4), (3, -5)$

14) through: $(0, 3), (1, 1)$

15) through: $(5, 5), (2, -3)$

16) through: $(-2, -2), (2, -5)$

17) through: $(-3, -2), (1, -1)$

18) through: $(-2, 1), (6, 5)$

Graphing Linear Inequalities

Helpful Hints

1– First, graph the "equals" line.

2– Choose a testing point. (it can be any point on both sides of the line.)

3– Put the value of (x, y) of that point in the inequality. If that works, that part of the line is the solution. If the values don't work, then the other part of the line is the solution.

✎ Sketch the graph of each linear inequality.

1) $y < -4x + 2$

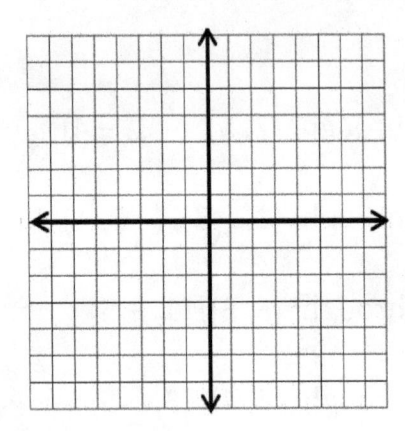

2) $2x + y < -4$

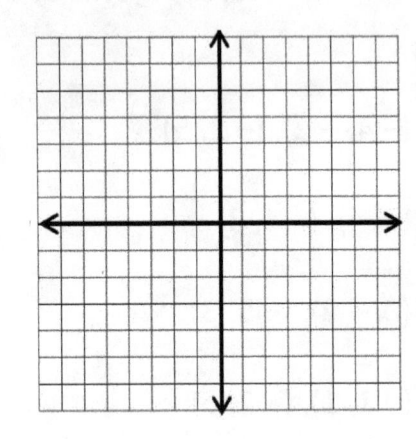

4) $x - 3y < -5$

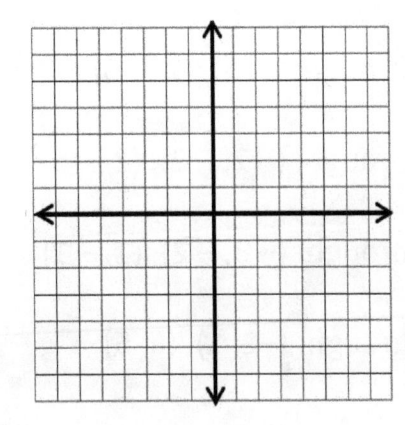

5) $6x - 2y \geq 8$

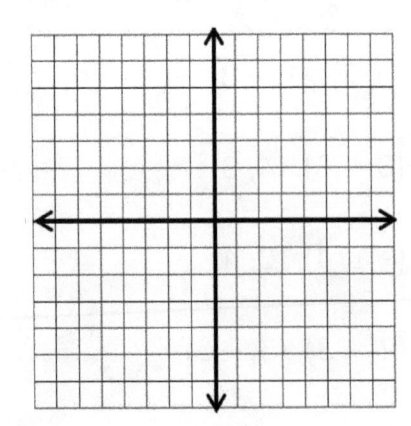

Finding Midpoint

Helpful Hints

Midpoint of the segment AB:

$$M\left(\frac{x_1+x_2}{2}, \frac{y_1+y_2}{2}\right)$$

Example:

(3, 9), (−1, 6)

M (1, 7.5)

✏️ *Find the midpoint of the line segment with the given endpoints.*

1) (2, −2), (3, −5)

2) (0, 2), (−2, −6)

3) (7, 4), (9, −1)

4) (4, −5), (0, 8)

5) (1, −2), (1, −6)

6) (−2, −3), (3, −6)

7) (7, 0), (−7, 5)

8) (−2, 6), (−3, −2)

9) (−1, 1), (5, −5)

10) (2.3, −1.3), (−2.2, −0.5)

11) (4.1, 6.32), (4, 5.6)

12) (2, −1), (−6, 0)

13) (−4, 4), (5, −1)

14) (−2, −3), (−6, 5)

15) ($\frac{1}{2}$, 1), (2, 4)

16) (−2, −2), (6, 5)

Finding Distance of Two Points

Helpful Hints

Distance from A to B:

$$d = \sqrt{(x_1 - x_2)^2 + (y_1 - y_2)^2}$$

Example:

$(-1, 2), (-1, -7)$

Distance = 9

✏️ **Find the distance between each pair of points.**

1) $(2, -1), (1, -1)$

2) $(6, 4), (-1, 3)$

3) $(-8, -5), (-6, 1)$

4) $(-6, -10), (-2, -10)$

5) $(4, -6), (-3, 4)$

6) $(-6, -7), (-2, -8)$

7) $(5, 4), (8, 2)$

8) $(8, 4), (3, -7)$

9) $(1, 3), (5, 7)$

10) $(4, 2), (-7, 1)$

11) $(-3, -4), (-7, -2)$

12) $(-7, -2), (6, 9)$

13) $(10, 0), (0, 4)$

14) $(-3, 2), (5, 0)$

15) $(-5, 6), (8, -4)$

16) $(3, -5), (-8, -4)$

17) $(0, 8), (4, 10)$

18) $(6, 4), (-5, -1)$

Slope and Rate of Change

> **Helpful Hints**
> - Slope can be described as "rate of change".
> - Rate of change is a ratio between a change in one variable comparing to a corresponding change in another variable.

Example:

Rate of change in the first graph is 1 and in the second graph is 1/3.

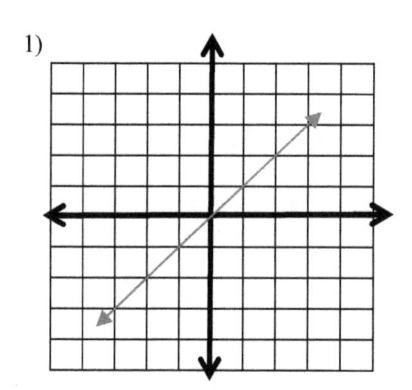

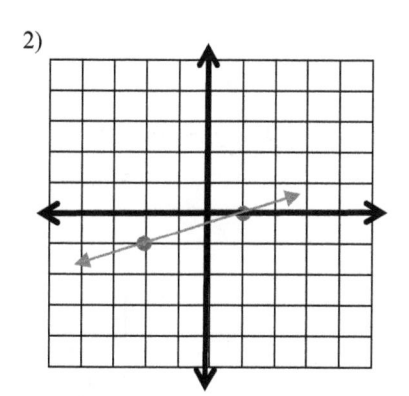

1)

2)

✏️ **Find the slope of the line that passes through the points.**

1) $(5, -2), (5, 8)$

2) $(1, 2), (7, 7)$

3) $(3, 0), (-5, -4)$

4) $(5, 9), (3, 9)$

5) $(12, 10), (12, 5)$

6) $(0.2, -0.9), (0.5, -0.9)$

7) $(7, -4), (4, 8)$

8) $(15, 2), (-6, 5)$

✏️ **Find the value of r so the line that passes through each pair of points has the given slope.**

9) $(r, 7), (11, 8), m = \frac{1}{3}$

10) $(-5, r), (1, 3), m = \frac{7}{6}$

11) $(-7, 2), (-8, r), m = 5$

12) $(r, 2), (5, r), m = 0$

Find the Slope, x–intercept and y–intercept

Helpful Hints

x-intercept: is a point in the equation where the value of y is zero.
y-intercept: is a point in the equation where the value of x is zero.

✎ *Find the x and y intercepts for the following equations.*

1) $x + 7y = 10$

2) $y = x + 3$

3) $4x = 2y + 6$

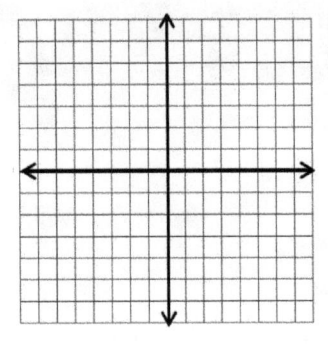

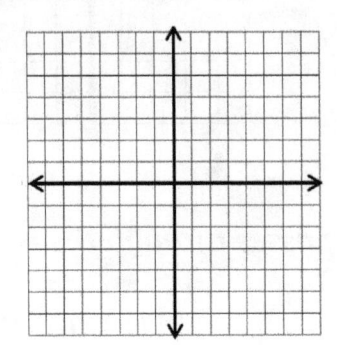

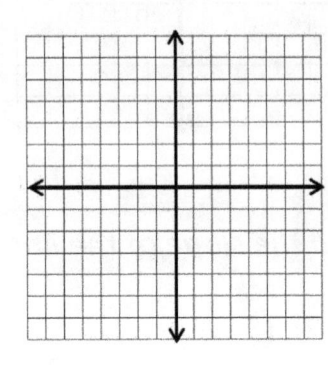

4) $5 - 2y = 3x$

5) $5x - 2y = 7$

6) $y = 4 + x$

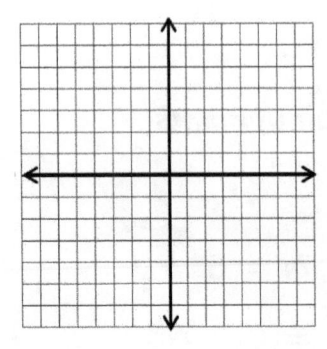

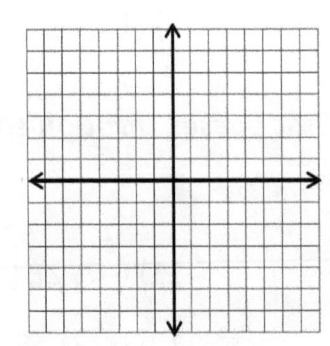

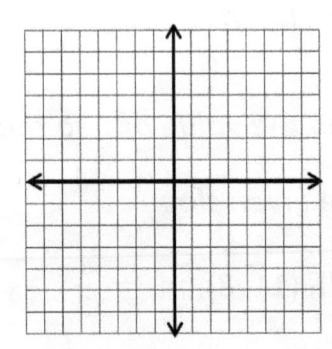

134

Write an Equation from a Graph

> **Helpful Hints**
>
> An equation in the slope-intercept form is written as
> $$y = mx + b$$
> Where m is the slope of the line and b is the y-intercept.

✎Write the slope intercept form of the equation of each line.

1)

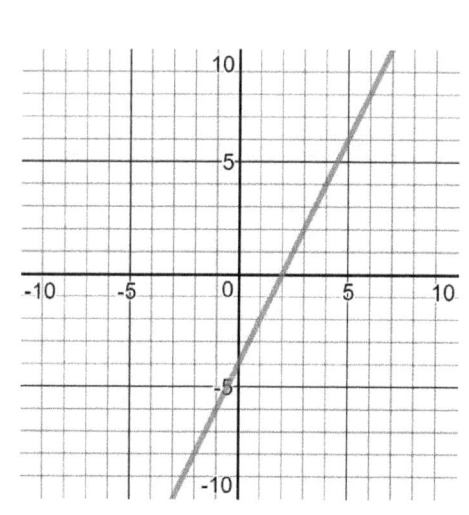

2)

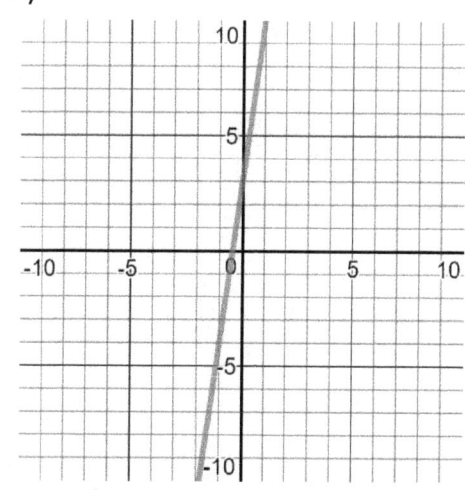

3)

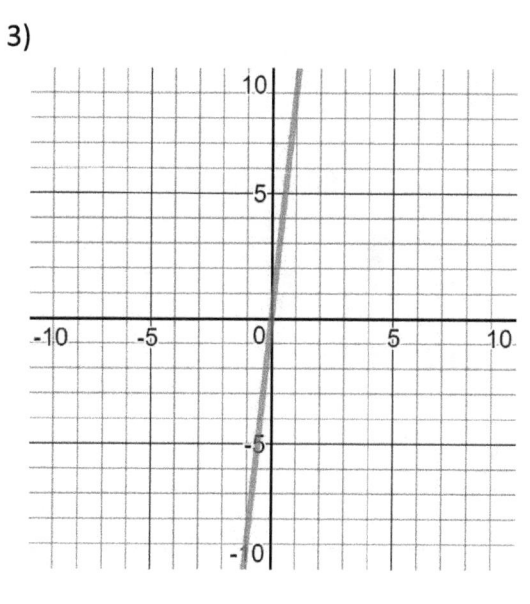

4)

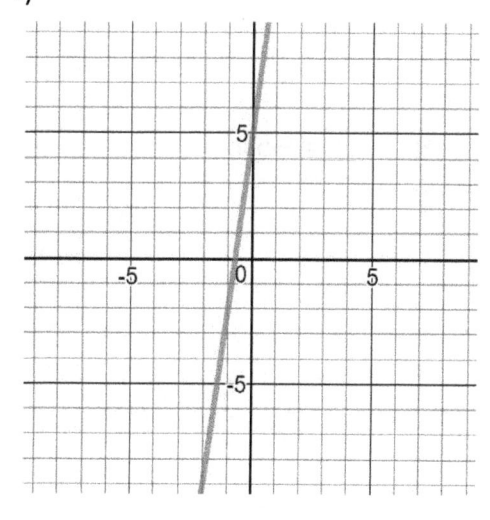

Slope–intercept Form

> **Helpful Hints**
>
> Using the slope m and the y-intercept b, then the equation of the line is:
>
> $$y = mx + b$$
>
> **Example:**
>
> $y = -10 + 2x$
>
> $m = 2$

✎ Write the slope–intercept form of the equation of each line.

1) $-14x + y = 7$

2) $-2(2x + y) = 28$

3) $-11x - 7y = -56$

4) $9x + 35 = -5y$

5) $x - 3y = 6$

6) $13x - 11y = -12$

7) $11x - 8y = -48$

8) $3x - 2y = -16$

9) $2y = -6x - 8$

10) $2y = -4x + 10$

11) $2y = -2x - 4$

12) $6x + 5y = -15$

136

Point–slope Form

> **Helpful Hints**
> Using the slope m and a point (x_1, y_1) on the line, the equation of the line is
> $(y - y_1) = m(x - x_1)$
>
> **Example:**
> $y = 2(x + 3)$
> $m = 2, (-3, 0)$

✏ *Find the slope of the following lines. Name a point on each line.*

1) $y = 2(x + 3)$

2) $y + 2 = \frac{2}{3}(x - 4)$

3) $y + 3 = -1.5x$

4) $y - 3 = \frac{1}{2}(x - 3)$

5) $y + 2 = 1.3(x + 1)$

6) $y - 5 = 3x$

7) $y - 3 = -2(x - 4)$

8) $y + 3 = 0$

9) $y + 2 = 3(x + 6)$

10) $y - 7 = -4(x - 2)$

✏ *Write an equation in point–slope form for the line that passes through the given point with the slope provided.*

11) $(1, 2)$, $m = 7$

12) $(3, 5)$, $m = \frac{5}{3}$

13) $(2, -4)$, $m = -1$

14) $(-1, 2)$, $m = 2$

15) $(-1, 4)$, $m = 4$

16) $(-1, 2)$, $m = 2$

17) $(3, 1)$, $m = \frac{1}{2}$

18) $(-2, 5)$, $m = -4$

Equations of Horizontal and Vertical Lines

Helpful Hints

The slope of horizontal lines is 0. Thus, the equation of horizontal lines becomes: $y = b$

The slope of vertical lines is undefined and the equation for a vertical line is: $x = a$

✏️ Sketch the graph of each line.

1) $y = 0$

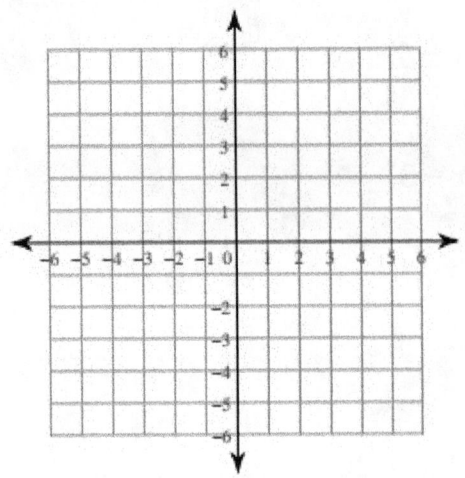

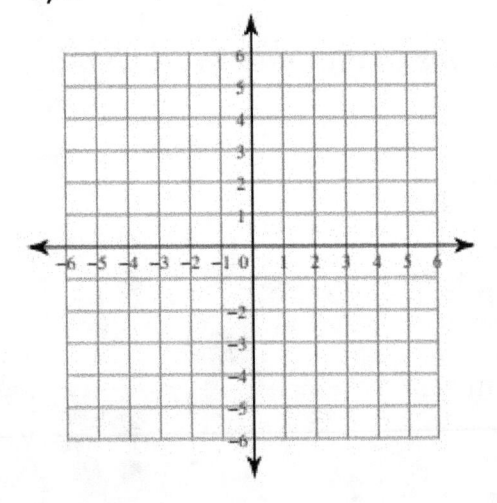

2) $y = 2$

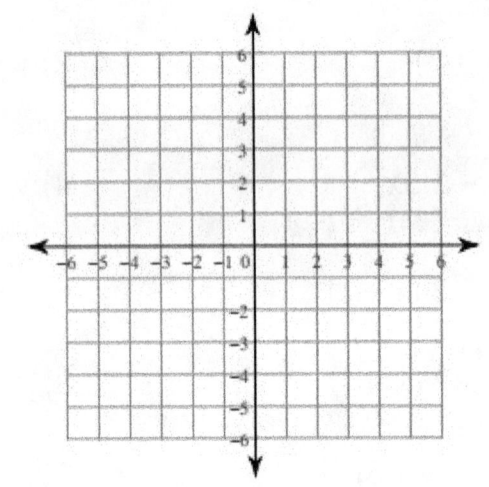

3) $x = -4$

4) $x = 3$

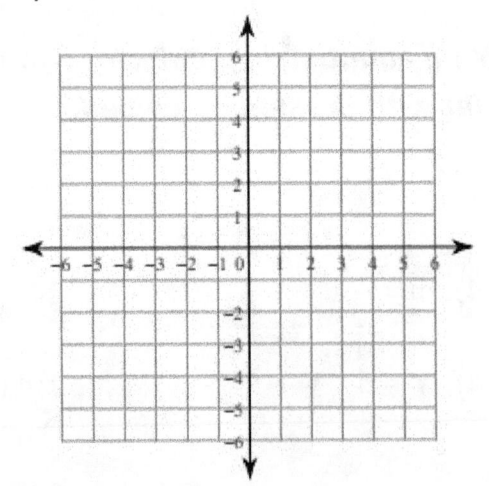

Equation of Parallel or Perpendicular Lines

> **Helpful Hints**
>
> **Parallel lines:** are distinct lines with the same slope. For example: if the following lines are parallel:
> $y = m_1x + b_1$
> $y = m_2x + b_2$
> Then, $m_1 = m_2$ and $b_1 \neq b_2$.
>
> **Perpendicular Lines:** A pair of lines is perpendicular if the lines meet at 90° angle.
> $y = m_1x + b_1$
> $y = m_2x + b_2$
> the two lines are perpendicular if, $m_1 = -\frac{1}{m_2}$, that is, if the slopes are negative reciprocals of each other.

✎ **Write an equation of the line that passes through the given point and is parallel to the given line.**

1) $(-2, -4)$, $4x + 7y = -14$

2) $(-4, 2)$, $y = -x + 3$

3) $(-2, 5)$, $2y = 4x - 6$

4) $(-10, 0)$, $-y + 3x = 16$

5) $(5, -1)$, $y = -\frac{3}{5}x - 3$

6) $(1, 7)$, $-6x + y = -1$

7) $(2, -3)$, $y = \frac{1}{5}x + 5$

8) $(1, 4)$, $-6x + 5y = -10$

9) $(3, -3)$, $y = -\frac{5}{2}x - 1$

10) $(-4, 3)$, $2x + 3y = -9$

✎ **Write an equation of the line that passes through the given point and is perpendicular to the given line.**

11) $(-1, -7)$, $3x + 12y = -6$

12) $(-3, 5)$, $5x - 6y = 9$

13) $(2, 6)$, $y = -3$

14) $(-2, 3)$, $x = 4$

15) $(1, -5)$, $y = \frac{1}{8}x + 2$

16) $(3, 4)$, $y = -2x - 4$

17) $(-5, 5)$, $y = \frac{5}{9}x - 4$

18) $(4, -1)$, $y = x + 2$

Test Preparation

1) Point A (−2, −8) and point B (13, 0) are located on a coordinate grid.

   Which measurement is closest to the distance between point A and point B?

   A. 8 units

   B. 13 units

   C. 15 units

   D. 17 units

2) Point A (−4, −8) and point B (1, 4) are located on a coordinate grid.

   Which measurement is closest to the distance between point A and point B?

   A. 8 units

   B. 13 units

   C. 15 units

   D. 17 units

3) In the xy-plane, the point $(4, 3)$ and $(3, 2)$ are on line A. Which of the following equations of lines is parallel to line A?

   A. $y = 3x$

   B. $y = \frac{x}{2}$

   C. $y = 2x$

   D. $y = x$

4) What is the x-intercept of the line with equation $2x - 2y = 5$?

   A. -5
   B. -2
   C. $\frac{5}{2}$
   D. $\frac{5}{4}$

Answers of Worksheets – Chapter 9

Finding Slope

1) 2
2) $\dfrac{2}{7}$
3) −11
4) 0
5) $-\dfrac{1}{32}$
6) 1
7) $-\dfrac{3}{2}$
8) −1
9) $-\dfrac{1}{3}$
10) $\dfrac{11}{2}$
11) $-\dfrac{1}{17}$
12) $-\dfrac{22}{23}$
13) $-\dfrac{3}{4}$
14) $-\dfrac{5}{8}$
15) $-\dfrac{1}{14}$
16) $\dfrac{11}{20}$
17) Undefined
18) $-\dfrac{3}{19}$

Graphing Lines Using Slope–Intercept Form

1)

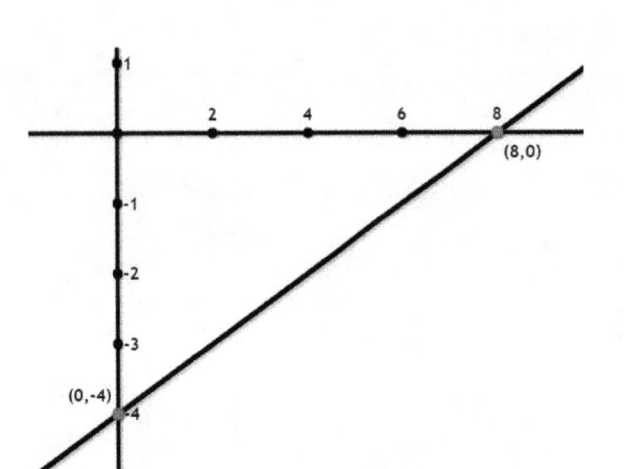

2)

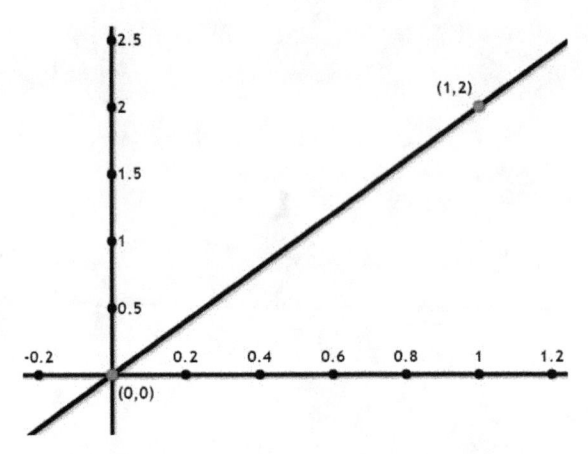

Graphing Lines Using Standard Form

1)

2)

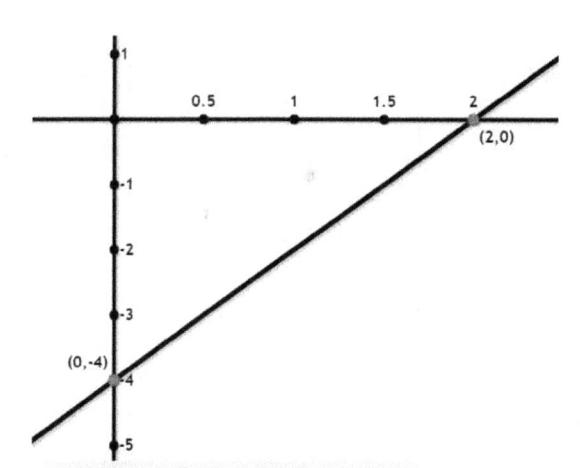

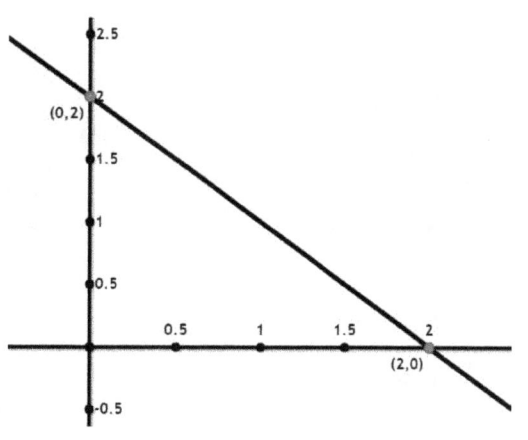

Writing Linear Equations

1) $y = 7x + 26$
2) $y = \frac{1}{9}x + \frac{31}{9}$
3) $y = -x - 2$
4) $y = -5x - 4$
5) $y = x + 3$
6) $y = -5x + 2$
7) $y = 2x - 5$
8) $y = 4$
9) $y = -2x + 1$
10) $y = 3x - 1$

11) $y = -x - 2$
12) $y = 4x - 9$
13) $y = 9x - 32$
14) $y = -2x + 3$
15) $y = \frac{8}{3}x - \frac{25}{3}$
16) $y = -\frac{3}{4}x - \frac{7}{2}$
17) $y = \frac{1}{4}x - \frac{5}{4}$
18) $y = -\frac{4}{3}x + \frac{19}{3}$

Graphing Linear Inequalities

1)

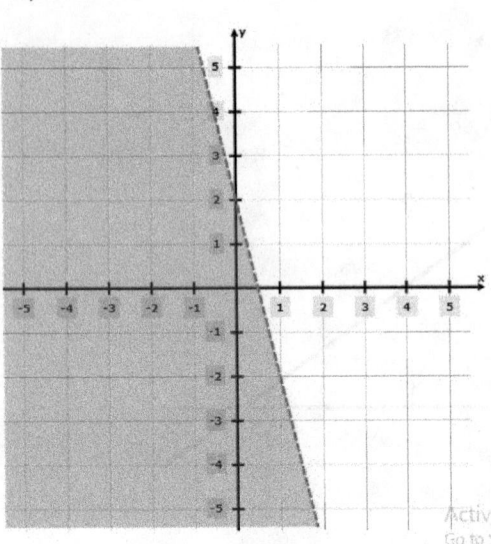

2)

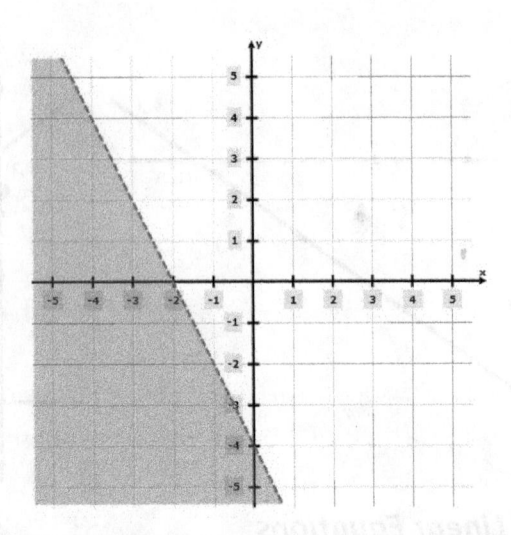

4)

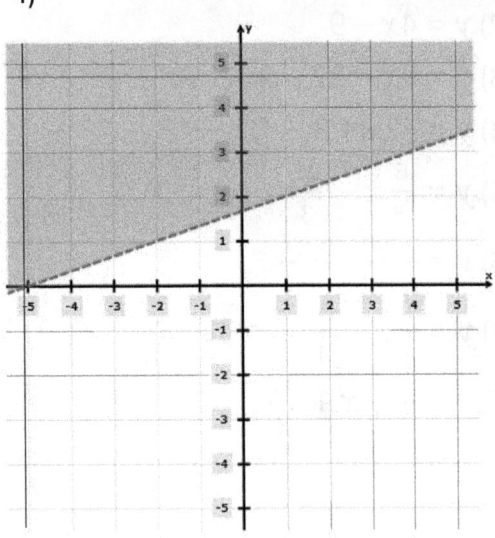

5)

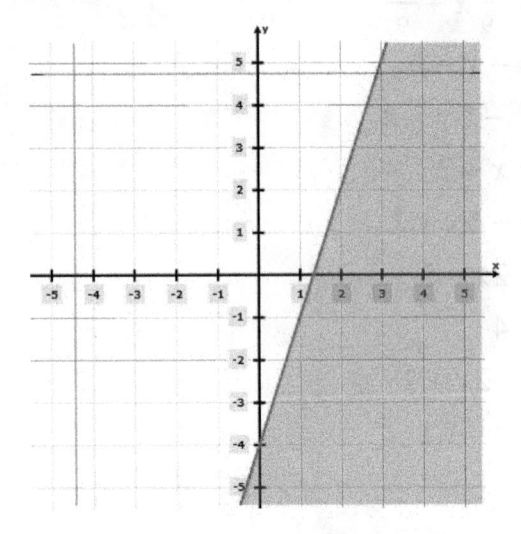

Finding Midpoint

1) (2.5, −3.5)
2) (−1, −2)
3) (8, 1.5)
4) (2, 1.5)
5) (1, −4)
6) (0.5, −4.5)
7) (0, 2.5)
8) (−2.5, 2)
9) (2, −2)
10) (0.05, −0.9)
11) (4.05, 5.96)
12) (−2, −0.5)
13) $(\frac{1}{2}, 1\frac{1}{2})$
14) (−4, 1)
15) (1.25, 2.5)
16) $(2, \frac{3}{2})$

Finding Distance of Two Points

1) 1
2) 7.1
3) 6.32
4) 4
5) 12.21
6) 4.12
7) 3.61
8) 12.1
9) 5.66
10) 11.04
11) 4.47
12) 17.03
13) 10.77
14) 8.25
15) 16.4
16) 10.3
17) 4.47
18) 12.1

Slope and Rate of Change

1) undefined
2) $\frac{5}{6}$
3) $\frac{1}{2}$
4) 0
5) undefined
6) 0
7) −4
8) $\frac{-1}{7}$
9) 8
10) −4
11) −3
12) 2

Find the Slope, x – intercept and y–intercept

1) y intercept = $\frac{10}{7}$
   x intercept = 10

2) y intercept = 3
   x intercept = –3

3) y intercept = –3
   x intercept = $\frac{3}{2}$

4) y intercept = $\frac{5}{2}$
   x intercept = $\frac{5}{3}$

5) y intercept = $-\frac{7}{2}$
   x intercept = $\frac{7}{5}$

6) y intercept = 4
   x intercept = –4

Write an equation from a graph

1) $y = 2x - 4$
2) $y = 7x + 3$
3) $y = 9x$
4) $y = 7x + 5$

Slope–intercept form

1) $y = 14x + 7$
2) $y = -2x - 14$
3) $y = -\frac{11}{7}x + 8$
4) $y = -\frac{9}{5}x - 7$
5) $y = \frac{x}{3} - 2$
6) $y = \frac{13}{11}x + \frac{12}{11}$
7) $y = \frac{11}{8}x + 6$
8) $y = \frac{3}{2}x + 8$
9) $y = -3x - 4$
10) $y = -2x + 5$
11) $y = -x - 2$
12) $y = -\frac{6}{5}x - 3$

Point–slope form

1) $m = 2, (-3, 0)$
2) $m = \frac{2}{3}, (4, -2)$
3) $m = -\frac{3}{2}, (0, -3)$
4) $m = \frac{1}{2}, (3, 3)$
5) $m = \frac{13}{10}, (-1, -2)$
6) $m = 3, (0, 5)$

FSA Mathematics Workbook For Grade 8

7) $m = -2$, (4, 3)

8) $m = 0$, (3, –3)

9) $m = 3$, (–6, –2)

10) $m = -4$, (2, 7)

11) $y - 2 = 7(x - 1)$

12) $y - 5 = \frac{5}{3}(x - 3) = 0$

13) $y + 4 = -(x - 2)$

14) $y - 2 = 2(x + 1)$

15) $y - 4 = 4(x + 1)$

16) $y - 2 = 2(x + 1)$

17) $y - 1 = \frac{1}{2}(x - 3)$

18) $y - 5 = -4(x + 2)$

Equations of horizontal and vertical lines

1) $y = 0$ (it is on x axes)

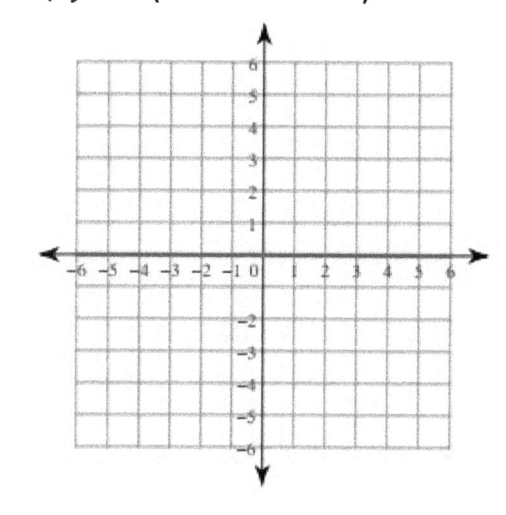

2) $y = 2$

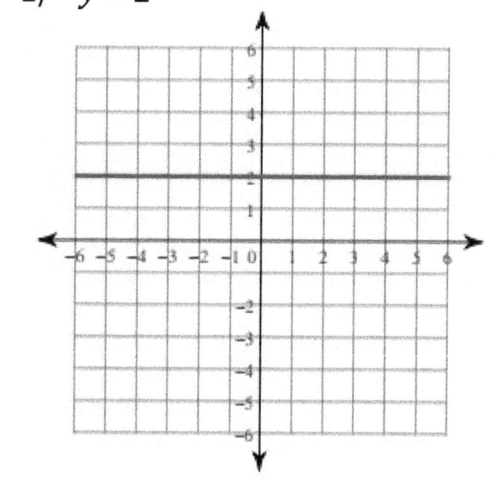

3) $x = -4$

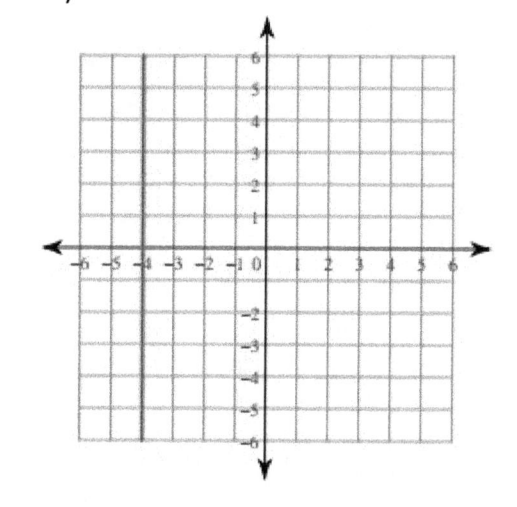

4) $x = 3$

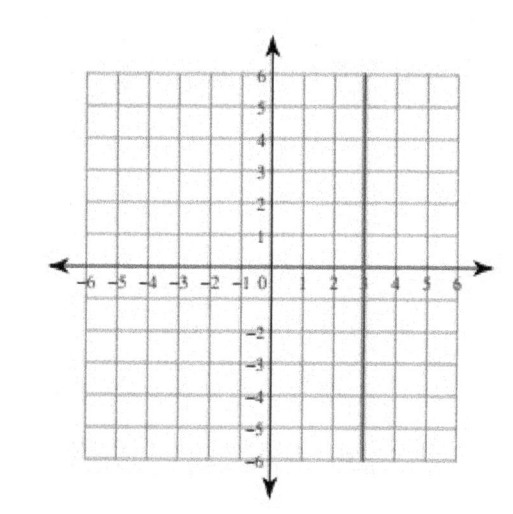

www.EffortlessMath.com

147

Equation of parallel or perpendicular lines

1) $y = -\frac{4}{7}x - \frac{36}{7}$

2) $y = -x - 2$

3) $y = 2x + 9$

4) $y = 3x + 30$

5) $y = -\frac{3}{5}x + 2$

6) $y = 6x + 1$

7) $y = \frac{1}{5}x - \frac{17}{5}$

8) $y = \frac{6}{5}x + \frac{14}{5}$

9) $y = -\frac{5}{2}x + \frac{9}{2}$

10) $y = -\frac{2}{3}x + \frac{1}{3}$

11) $y = 4x - 3$

12) $y = -\frac{6}{5}x + \frac{7}{5}$

13) $x = 2$

14) $y = 3$

15) $y = -8x + 3$

16) $y = \frac{1}{2}x + \frac{5}{2}$

17) $y = -\frac{9}{5}x - 4$

18) $y = -x + 3$

148

Test Preparation Answers

1) Choice D is correct.

Distance between two points = $\sqrt{(x_1 - x_2)^2 + (y_1 - y_2)^2}$
$\sqrt{(-2 - 13)^2 + (-8 - 0)^2} = \sqrt{(-15)^2 + (-8)^2} = \sqrt{289} = 17$

2) Choice B is correct

Distance between two points = $\sqrt{(x_1 - x_2)^2 + (y_1 - y_2)^2}$
$\sqrt{(-4 - 1)^2 + (-8 - 4)^2} = \sqrt{(-5)^2 + (-12)^2} = \sqrt{169} = 13$

3) Choice D is correct

The slop of line A is: $m = \frac{y_2 - y_1}{x_2 - x_1} = \frac{3-2}{4-3} = 1$

Parallel lines have the same slope and only choice D ($y = x$) has slope of 1.

4) Choice C is correct

The value of y in the x-intercept of a line is zero. Then:

$y = 0 \rightarrow 2x - 2(0) = 5 \rightarrow 2x = 5 \rightarrow x = \frac{5}{2}$

then, x-intercept of the line is $\frac{5}{2}$

Chapter 10: Monomials and Polynomials

Topics that you'll learn in this chapter:

- ✓ Classifying Polynomials
- ✓ Writing Polynomials in Standard Form
- ✓ Simplifying Polynomials
- ✓ Add and Subtract Monomials
- ✓ Multiplying Monomials
- ✓ Multiplying and Dividing Monomials
- ✓ GCF of Monomials
- ✓ Powers of Monomials
- ✓ Multiplying a Polynomial and a Monomial
- ✓ Multiplying Binomials
- ✓ Factoring Trinomials

Classifying Polynomials

Helpful Hints

Name	Degree	Example
constant	0	4
linear	1	$2x$
quadratic	2	$x^2 + 5x + 6$
cubic	3	$x^3 - x^2 + 4x + 8$
quartic	4	$x^4 + 3x^3 - x^2 + 2x + 6$
quantic	5	$x^5 - 2x^4 + x^3 - x^2 + x + 10$

Name each polynomial by degree and number of terms.

1) x

2) $-5x^4$

3) $7x - 4$

4) -6

5) $8x + 1$

6) $9x^2 - 8x^3$

7) $2x^5$

8) $10 + 8x$

9) $5x^2 - 6x$

10) $-7x^7 + 7x^4$

11) $-8x^4 + 5x^3 - 2x^2 - 8x$

12) $4x - 9x^2 + 4x^3 - 5x^4$

13) $4x^6 + 5x^5 + x^4$

14) $-4 - 2x^2 + 8x$

15) $9x^6 - 8$

16) $7x^5 + 10x^4 - 3x + 10x^7$

17) $4x^6 - 3x^2 - 8x^4$

18) $-5x^4 + 10x - 10$

Writing Polynomials in Standard Form

Helpful Hints

A polynomial function $f(x)$ of degree n is of the form
$f(x) = a_n x^n + a_{n-1} x^{n-1} + \ldots + a_1 x + a_0$
The first term is the one with the biggest power!

Example:
$2x^2 - 4x^3 - x =$
$-4x^3 + 2x^2 - x$

Write each polynomial in standard form.

1) $3x^2 - 5x^3$

2) $3 + 4x^3 - 3$

3) $2x^2 + 1x - 6x^3$

4) $9x - 7x$

5) $12 - 7x + 9x^4$

6) $5x^2 + 13x - 2x^3$

7) $-3 + 16x - 16x$

8) $3x(x + 4) - 2(x + 4)$

9) $(x + 5)(x - 2)$

10) $3x^2 + x + 12 - 5x^2 - 2x$

11) $12x^5 + 7x^3 - 3x^5 - 8x^3$

12) $3x(2x + 5 - 2x^2)$

13) $11x(x^5 + 2x^3)$

14) $(x + 6)(x + 3)$

15) $(x + 4)^2$

16) $(8x - 7)(3x + 2)$

17) $5x(3x^2 + 2x + 1)$

18) $7x(3 - x + 6x^3)$

Simplifying Polynomials

> **Helpful Hints**
>
> 1- Find "like" terms. (they have same variables with same power).
> 2- Add or Subtract "like" terms using PEMDAS operation.
>
> **Example:**
> $2x^5 - 3x^3 + 8x^2 - 2x^5 =$
> $-3x^3 + 8x^2$

Simplify each expression.

1) $11 - 4x^2 + 3x^2 - 7x^3 + 3$

2) $2x^5 - x^3 + 8x^2 - 2x^5$

3) $(-5)(x^6 + 10) - 8(14 - x^6)$

4) $4(2x^2 + 4x^2 - 3x^3) + 6x^3 + 17$

5) $11 - 6x^2 + 5x^2 - 12x^3 + 22$

6) $2x^2 - 2x + 3x^3 + 12x - 22x$

7) $(3x - 8)(3x - 4)$

8) $(12x + 2y)^2$

9) $(12x^3 + 28x^2 + 10x + 4) \div (x + 2)$

10) $(2x + 12x^2 - 2) \div (x + 2)$

11) $(2x^3 - 1) + (3x^3 - 2x^3)$

12) $(x - 5)(x - 3)$

13) $(3x + 8)(3x - 8)$

14) $(8x^2 - 3x) - (5x - 5 - 8x^2)$

FSA Mathematics Workbook For Grade 8

Add and Subtract monomials

Helpful Hints

A monomial is a number, a variable or a product of a number and a variable where all exponents are whole numbers.

Example:
$5u^2v + 6u^2v = 11u^2v$

$xyz + (-6xyz) = 5xyz$

Find each sum and difference.

1) $5u^2v + 6u^2v$

2) $xyz + (-6xyz)$

3) $10u + (-2u)$

4) $12xy + xy$

5) $15y - 12y$

6) $(-5x) + (-7x)$

7) $(-40x) - 14x$

8) $56x^2 + 31x^2$

9) $y^4 - (-6y^4)$

10) $25x^3 + 75x^3$

11) $5xy^2z + (-7xy^2z)$

12) $5x^2yz^2 + 8x^2yz^2$

13) $6y^6 - (-15y^6)$

14) $2x^2 - (-8x^2)$

15) $(-6pqr) + 3pqr$

16) $8x^4y - 6x^4y$

17) $18r^2t^4 + 26r^2t^4$

18) $51x^2yz^2 - 21x^2yz^2$

Multiplying Monomials

Helpful Hints

A monomial is a polynomial with just one term, like $2x$ or $7y$.

Example:
$2u^3 \times (-3u)$
$= -6u^4$

Simplify each expression.

1) $2xy^2z \times 4z^2$

2) $4xy \times x^2y$

3) $4pq^3 \times (-2p^4q)$

4) $8s^4t^2 \times st^5$

5) $12p^3 \times (-3p^4)$

6) $-4p^2q^3r \times 6pq^2r^3$

7) $(-8a^4) \times (-12a^6b)$

8) $3u^4v^2 \times (-7u^2v^3)$

9) $4u^3 \times (-2u)$

10) $-6xy^2 \times 3x^2y$

11) $12y^2z^3 \times (-y^2z)$

12) $5a^2bc^2 \times 2abc^2$

155

Multiplying and Dividing Monomials

Helpful Hints
- When you divide two monomials you need to divide their coefficients and then divide their variables.
- In case of exponents with the same base, you need to subtract their powers.

Simplify.

1) $(-3x^2)(8x^4y^{12})$

2) $(7x^4y^6)(4x^3y^4)$

3) $(15x^4)(3x^9)$

4) $(12x^2y^9)(7x^9y^{12})$

5) $\dfrac{36\,x^5y^7}{4\,x^4y^5}$

6) $\dfrac{80\,x^{12}y^9}{10\,x^6y^7}$

7) $\dfrac{95\,x^{18}y^7}{5\,x^9y^2}$

8) $\dfrac{200\,x^3y^8}{40\,x^3y^7}$

9) $\dfrac{-15\,x^{17}y^{13}}{3\,x^6y^9}$

10) $\dfrac{-64\,x^8y^{10}}{8\,x^3y^7}$

GCF of Monomials

Helpful Hints

To find the greatest common factor of two monomials, find the prime factorization of each monomial. Then take the product of all common factors.

Example:
GCF of:
$54x^3, 36x^3 = 18x^3$
$33x, 44y^2x = 11x$

Find the GCF of each set of monomials.

1) $54x^3, 36x^3$

2) $33x, 44y^2x$

3) $15x^2, 12, 48$

4) $10v^3, 45v^3, 35v$

5) p^2q^2, pqr

6) $15m^2n, 25m^2n^2$

7) $12x^2yz, 3xy^2$

8) $22m^5n^2, 11m^2n^4$

9) $16x^3y, 8x^2$

10) $14ab^5, 7a^2b^2c$

11) $12t^7u^2, 18t^3u^7$

12) $18t, 48t^4$

13) $18r^3t, 26qr^2t^4$

14) $11a^4b^3, 44a^2b^5$

15) $16f, 21ab^2$

16) $12a^2b^2c^2, 20abc$

17) $18ab, 9ab$

18) $22m^5n^2, 11m^2n^4$

19) $4xy, 2x^2$

20) $x^3yz^2, 2x^3yz^3$

Powers of monomials

Helpful Hints

For any nonzero numbers a and b and any integer x,
$(ab)^x = a^x \cdot b^x$.

Example:
$(2x^2 \cdot y^3)^2 = 4x^2 \cdot y^6$

Simplify.

1) $(3x^4)^7$

2) $(4y^2 2y^3 y)^2$

3) $(3x^2 2x^2)^3$

4) $(8x^4 y^3)^6$

5) $(3y^2 5y^2)^2$

6) $(6x^3 y)^3$

7) $(8x^2 x^2 3n)^2$

8) $(7xy^6)^3$

9) $(9x^3 y^2)^4$

10) $(10y^3 y^2)^3$

11) $(6x^2 x^6)^3$

12) $(3x^7 4x^3 k^2)^2$

13) $(4y^5 4y^2)^2$

14) $(5x 2x^3)^3$

15) $(4y^3)^3$

16) $(y^3 y^3 y^2)^3$

17) $(4y^2 y)^3$

18) $(6xy^6)^3$

Multiplying a Polynomial and a Monomial

Helpful Hints
- When multiplying monomials, use the product rule for exponents.
- When multiplying a monomial by a polynomial, use the distributive property.
$a \times (b + c) = a \times b + a \times c$

Example:
$2x(8x - 2) =$
$16x^2 - 4x$

Find each product.

1) $5(3x - 6y)$

2) $9x(2x + 4y)$

3) $8x(7x - 4)$

4) $12x(3x + 9)$

5) $11x(2x - 11y)$

6) $2x(6x - 6y)$

7) $3x(2x^2 - 3x + 8)$

8) $13x(4x + 8y)$

9) $20(2x^2 - 8x - 5)$

10) $3x(3x - 2)$

11) $6x^3(3x^2 - 2x + 2)$

12) $8x^2(3x^2 - 5xy + 7y^2)$

13) $2x^2(3x^2 - 5x + 12)$

14) $2x^3(2x^2 + 5x - 4)$

15) $5x(6x^2 - 5xy + 2y^2)$

16) $9(x^2 + xy - 8y^2)$

Multiplying Binomials

Helpful Hints

Use "FOIL". (First-Out-In-Last)

$(x + a)(x + b) = x^2 + (b + a)x + ab$

Example:
$(x + 2)(x - 3) = x^2 - x - 6$

Simplify each expression.

1) $(3x - 2)(4x + 2)$

2) $(2x - 5)(x + 7)$

3) $(x + 2)(x + 8)$

4) $(x^2 + 2)(x^2 - 2)$

5) $(x - 2)(x + 4)$

6) $(x - 8)(2x + 8)$

7) $(5x - 4)(3x + 3)$

8) $(x - 7)(x - 6)$

9) $(6x + 9)(4x + 9)$

10) $(2x - 6)(5x + 6)$

11) $(x - 7)(x + 7)$

12) $(x + 4)(4x - 8)$

13) $(6x - 4)(6x + 4)$

14) $(x - 7)(x + 2)$

15) $(x - 8)(x + 8)$

16) $(3x + 3)(3x - 4)$

17) $(x + 3)(x + 3)$

18) $(x + 4)(x + 6)$

Factoring Trinomials

Helpful Hints

"FOIL"
$(x + a)(x + b) = x^2 + (b + a)x + ab$

"Difference of Squares"
$a^2 - b^2 = (a + b)(a - b)$
$a^2 + 2ab + b^2 = (a + b)(a + b)$
$a^2 - 2ab + b^2 = (a - b)(a - b)$

"Reverse FOIL"
$x^2 + (b + a)x + ab = (x + a)(x + b)$

Example:
$x^2 + 5x + 6 =$
$(x + 2)(x + 3)$.

Factor each trinomial.

1) $x^2 - 7x + 12$

2) $x^2 + 5x - 14$

3) $x^2 - 11x - 42$

4) $6x^2 + x - 12$

5) $x^2 - 17x + 30$

6) $x^2 + 8x + 15$

7) $3x^2 + 11x - 4$

8) $x^2 - 6x - 27$

9) $10x^2 + 33x - 7$

10) $x^2 + 24x + 144$

11) $49x^2 + 28xy + 4y^2$

12) $16x^2 - 40x + 25$

13) $x^2 - 10x + 25$

14) $25x^2 - 20x + 4$

15) $x^3 + 6x^2y^2 + 9xy^3$

16) $9x^2 + 24x + 16$

17) $x^2 - 8x + 16$

18) $x^2 + 121 + 22x$

Test Preparation

1) Simplify $6x^2y^3(2x^2y)^3 =$

    A. $12x^4y^6$

    B. $12x^8y^6$

    C. $48x^4y^6$

    D. $48x^8y^6$

2) Both $(x = -2)$ and $(x = 3)$ are solutions for which of the following equations?

    I. $x^2 - x + 6 = 0$

    II. $2x^2 - 2x = 12$

    III. $5x^2 - 5x - 30 = 0$

    A. II only

    B. I and II

    C. II and III

    D. I, II and III

3) If $(x - 2)^3 = 27$ which of the following could be the value of $(x - 4)(x - 3)$?

A. 1
B. 2
C. −1
D. −2

4) If $x \neq 0$, what is the value of $\frac{(10(x)(y^2))^2}{(8xy^2)^2}$?

5) If $x^2 + 6x - r$ is divisible by $(x - 5)$, what is the value of r?

A. 55
B. 56
C. 57
D. 58

Answers of Worksheets – Chapter 10

Classifying Polynomials

1) Linear monomial
2) Quartic monomial
3) Linear binomial
4) Constant monomial
5) Linear binomial
6) Cubic binomial
7) Quantic monomial
8) Linear binomial
9) Quadratic binomial
10) Seventh degree binomial
11) Quartic polynomial with four terms
12) Quartic polynomial with four terms
13) Sixth degree trinomial
14) Quadratic trinomial
15) Sixth degree binomial
16) Seventh degree polynomial with four terms
17) Sixth degree trinomial
18) Quartic trinomial

Writing Polynomials in Standard Form

1) $-5x^3 + 3x^2$
2) $4x^3$
3) $-6x^3 + 2x^2 + x$
4) $2x$
5) $9x^4 - 7x + 12$
6) $-2x^3 + 5x^2 + 13x$
7) -3
8) $3x^2 + 10x - 8$
9) $x^2 + 3x - 10$
10) $-2x^2 - x + 12$
11) $9x^5 - x^3$
12) $-6x^3 + 6x^2 + 15x$
13) $11x^6 + 22x^4$
14) $x^2 + 9x + 18$
15) $x^2 + 8x + 16$
16) $24x^2 - 5x - 14$
17) $15x^3 + 10x^2 + 5x$
18) $42x^4 - 7x^2 + 21x$

Simplifying Polynomials

1) $-7x^3 - x^2 + 14$
2) $-3x^3 + 8x^2$
3) $3x^6 - 162$
4) $-6x^3 + 24x^2 + 17$
5) $-12x^3 - x^2 + 33$
6) $3x^3 + 2x^2 - 12x$
7) $9x^2 - 36x + 32$
8) $144x^2 + 48xy + 4y^2$
9) $12x^2 + 4x + 2$
10) $12x - 22 + \frac{42}{x+2}$
11) $3x^3 - 1$
12) $x^2 - 8x + 15$
13) $9x^2 - 64$
14) $16x^2 - 8x + 5$

Add and Subtract Monomials

1) $11u^2v$
2) $5xyz$
3) $8u$
4) $13xy$
5) $13y$
6) $-12x$
7) $-54x$
8) $87x^2$
9) $7y^4$
10) $100x^3$
11) $-2xy^2z$
12) $13x^2yz^2$
13) $21y^6$
14) $10x^2$
15) $-3pqr$
16) $2x^4y$
17) $44r^2t^4$
18) $30x^2yz^2$

Multiplying Monomials

1) $8xy^2z^3$
2) $4x^3y^2$
3) $-8p^5q^4$
4) $8s^5t^7$
5) $-36p^7$
6) $-24p^3q^5r^4$
7) $96a^{10}b$
8) $-21u^6v^5$
9) $-8u^4$
10) $-18x^3y^3$
11) $-12y^4z^4$
12) $10a^3b^2c^4$

Multiplying and Dividing Monomials

1) $-24x^6y^{12}$
2) $28x^7y^{10}$
3) $45x^{13}$
4) $84x^{11}y^{21}$
5) $9xy^2$
6) $8x^6y^2$
7) $19x^9y^5$
8) $5y$
9) $-5x^{11}y^4$
10) $-8x^5y^3$

GCF of monomials

1) $18x^3$
2) $11x$
3) 3
4) $5v$
5) pq
6) $5m^2n$
7) $3xy$
8) $11m^2n$
9) $8x^2$
10) $7ab^2$
11) $6t^3u^2$
12) $8t$
13) $2r^2t$
14) $11a^2b^3$
15) no
16) $4abc$
17) $9ab$
18) $11m^2n^2$
19) $2x$
20) x^3yz^2

Powers of monomials

1) $2187x^{28}$
2) $72x^{12}$
3) $216x^{12}$
4) $262144x^{24}y^{18}$
5) $225y^{10}$
6) $216x^9y^3$
7) $576x^8n^2$
8) $343x^3y^{18}$
9) $6561x^{12}y^8$
10) $1000y^{15}$
11) $396x^{24}$
12) $144x^{100}k^4$
13) $256y^{14}$
14) $1000x^{12}$
15) $64y^9$
16) $27y^{18}$
17) $64y^9$
18) $216x^3y^{18}$

Multiplying a Polynomial and a Monomial

1) $15x - 30y$
2) $18x^2 + 36xy$
3) $56x^2 - 32x$
4) $36x^2 + 108x$
5) $22x^2 - 121xy$
6) $12x^2 - 12xy$

7) $6x^3 - 9x^2 + 24x$
8) $52x^2 + 104xy$
9) $40x^2 - 160x - 100$
10) $9x^2 - 6x$
11) $18x^5 - 12x^4 + 12x^3$

12) $24x^4 - 40x^3y + 56y^2x^2$
13) $6x^4 - 10x^3 + 24x^2$
14) $4x^5 + 10x^4 - 8x^3$
15) $30x^3 - 25x^2y + 10xy^2$
16) $9x^2 + 9xy - 72y^2$

Multiplying Binomials

1) $12x^2 - 2x - 4$
2) $2x^2 + 9x - 35$
3) $x^2 + 10x + 16$
4) $x^4 - 4$
5) $x^2 + 2x - 8$
6) $2x^2 - 8x - 64$
7) $15x^2 + 3x - 12$
8) $x^2 - 13x + 42$
9) $24x^2 + 90x + 81$

10) $10x^2 - 18x - 36$
11) $x^2 - 49$
12) $4x^2 + 8x - 32$
13) $36x^2 - 16$
14) $x^2 - 5x - 14$
15) $x^2 - 64$
16) $9x^2 - 3x - 12$
17) $x^2 + 6x + 9$
18) $x^2 + 10x + 24$

Factoring Trinomials

1) $(x - 3)(x - 4)$
2) $(x - 2)(x + 7)$
3) $(x + 3)(x - 14)$
4) $(2x + 3)(3x - 4)$
5) $(x - 15)(x - 2)$
6) $(x + 3)(x + 5)$
7) $(3x + 1)(x - 4)$
8) $(x - 9)(x + 3)$
9) $(5x - 1)(2x + 7)$

10) $(x + 12)(x + 12)$
11) $(7x + 2y)(7x + 2y)$
12) $(4x - 5)(4x - 5)$
13) $(x - 5)(x - 5)$
14) $(5x - 2)(5x - 2)$
15) $x(x^2 + 6xy^2 + 9y^3)$
16) $(3x + 4)(3x + 4)$
17) $(x - 4)(x - 4)$
18) $(x + 11)(x + 11)$

Test Preparation Answers

1) Choice D is correct

Simplify.

$6x^2y^3(2x^2y)^3 = 6x^2y^3(8x^6y^3) = 48x^8y^6$

2) Choice C is correct

Plug in the values of x in each equation and check.

I. $(-2)^2 - 2 + 6 = 4 - 2 + 6 = 8 \neq 0$

      $(3)^2 - 3 + 6 = 3 - 3 + 6 = 12 \neq 0$

II. $2(-2)^2 - 2(-2) = 8 + 4 = 12 \rightarrow 12 = 12$

     $2(3)^2 - 2(3) = 18 - 6 = 12 \rightarrow 12 = 12$

III. $5(-2)^2 - 5(-2) - 30 = 20 + 10 - 30 = 0$

     $5(3)^2 - 5(3) - 30 = 45 - 15 - 30 = 0$

Equations II and III are correct.

3) Choice B is correct

$(x - 2)^3 = 27 \rightarrow$ Find the third root of both sides. Then:

$x - 2 = 3 \rightarrow x = 5$

$\rightarrow (x - 4)(x - 3) = (5 - 4)(5 - 3) = (1)(2) = 2$

4) The answer is $\frac{25}{16}$.

First, simplify the numerator and the denominator.

$$\frac{(10(x)(y^2)^2}{(8xy^2)^2} = \frac{100x^2y^4}{64x^2y^4}$$

Remove x^2y^4 from both numerator and denominator.

$$\frac{100x^2y^4}{64x^2y^4} = \frac{100}{64} = \frac{25}{16}$$

5) Choice A is correct

If $r = 55 \to \frac{x^2+6x-55}{x-5} = \frac{(x+11)(x-5)}{(x-5)} = x + 11$

For all other options, the numerator expression is not divisible by $(x-5)$.

Chapter 11: Exponents and Radicals

Topics that you'll learn in this chapter:

- ✓ Multiplication Property of Exponents
- ✓ Division Property of Exponents
- ✓ Powers of Products and Quotients
- ✓ Zero and Negative Exponents
- ✓ Negative Exponents and Negative Bases
- ✓ Writing Scientific Notation
- ✓ Square Roots

Multiplication Property of Exponents

Helpful Hints

Exponents rules

$x^a \cdot x^b = x^{a+b}$ $x^a/x^b = x^{a-b}$

$1/x^b = x^{-b}$ $(x^a)^b = x^{a \cdot b}$

$(xy)^a = x^a \cdot y^a$

Example:

$(x^2y)^3 = x^6y^3$

Simplify.

1) $4^2 \cdot 4^2$

2) $2 \cdot 2^2 \cdot 2^2$

3) $3^2 \cdot 3^2$

4) $3x^3 \cdot x$

5) $12x^4 \cdot 3x$

6) $6x \cdot 2x^2$

7) $5x^4 \cdot 5x^4$

8) $6x^2 \cdot 6x^3y^4$

9) $7x^2y^5 \cdot 9xy^3$

10) $7xy^4 \cdot 4x^3y^3$

11) $(2x^2)^2$

12) $3x^5y^3 \cdot 8x^2y^3$

13) $7x^3 \cdot 10y^3x^5 \cdot 8yx^3$

14) $(x^4)^3$

15) $(2x^2)^4$

16) $(x^2)^3$

17) $(6x)^2$

18) $3x^4y^5 \cdot 7x^2y^3$

Division Property of Exponents

Helpful Hints

$\dfrac{x^a}{x^b} = x^{a-b}, x \neq 0$

Example:

$\dfrac{x^{12}}{x^5} = x^7$

Simplify.

1) $\dfrac{5^5}{5}$

2) $\dfrac{3}{3^5}$

3) $\dfrac{2^2}{2^3}$

4) $\dfrac{2^4}{2^2}$

5) $\dfrac{x}{x^3}$

6) $\dfrac{3x^3}{9x^4}$

7) $\dfrac{2x^{-5}}{9x^{-2}}$

8) $\dfrac{21x^8}{7x^3}$

9) $\dfrac{7x^6}{4x^7}$

10) $\dfrac{6x^2}{4x^3}$

11) $\dfrac{5x}{10x^3}$

12) $\dfrac{3x^3}{2x^5}$

13) $\dfrac{12x^3}{14x^6}$

14) $\dfrac{12x^3}{9y^8}$

15) $\dfrac{25xy^4}{5x^6y^2}$

16) $\dfrac{2x^4}{7x}$

17) $\dfrac{16x^2y^8}{4x^3}$

18) $\dfrac{12x^4}{15x^7y^9}$

19) $\dfrac{12yx^4}{10yx^8}$

20) $\dfrac{16x^4y}{9x^8y^2}$

21) $\dfrac{5x^8}{20x^8}$

Powers of Products and Quotients

Helpful Hints

For any nonzero numbers a and b and any integer x, $(ab)^x = a^x \cdot b^x$.

Example:

$(2x^2 \cdot y^3)^2 =$

$4x^2 \cdot y^6$

✎ Simplify.

1) $(2x^3)^4$

2) $(4xy^4)^2$

3) $(5x^4)^2$

4) $(11x^5)^2$

5) $(4x^2y^4)^4$

6) $(2x^4y^4)^3$

7) $(3x^2y^2)^2$

8) $(3x^4y^3)^4$

9) $(2x^6y^8)^2$

10) $(12x\ 3x)^3$

11) $(2x^9\ x^6)^3$

12) $(5x^{10}y^3)^3$

13) $(4x^3\ x^2)^2$

14) $(3x^3\ 5x)^2$

15) $(10x^{11}y^3)^2$

16) $(9x^7\ y^5)^2$

17) $(4x^4y^6)^5$

18) $(4x^4)^2$

19) $(3x\ 4y^3)^2$

20) $(9x^2y)^3$

21) $(12x^2y^5)^2$

Zero and Negative Exponents

Helpful Hints

A negative exponent simply means that the base is on the wrong side of the fraction line, so you need to flip the base to the other side. For instance, "x^{-2}" (pronounced as "ecks to the minus two") just means "x^2" but underneath, as in $\frac{1}{x^2}$

Example:

$5^{-2} = \frac{1}{25}$

✎ Evaluate the following expressions.

1) 8^{-2}

2) 2^{-4}

3) 10^{-2}

4) 5^{-3}

5) 22^{-1}

6) 9^{-1}

7) 3^{-2}

8) 4^{-2}

9) 5^{-2}

10) 35^{-1}

11) 6^{-3}

12) 0^{15}

13) 10^{-9}

14) 3^{-4}

15) 5^{-2}

16) 2^{-3}

17) 3^{-3}

18) 8^{-1}

19) 7^{-3}

20) 6^{-2}

21) $\left(\frac{2}{3}\right)^{-2}$

22) $\left(\frac{1}{5}\right)^{-3}$

23) $\left(\frac{1}{2}\right)^{-8}$

24) $\left(\frac{2}{5}\right)^{-3}$

Negative Exponents and Negative Bases

Helpful Hints

– Make the power positive. A negative exponent is the reciprocal of that number with a positive exponent.

– The parenthesis is important!

-5^{-2} is not the same as $(-5)^{-2}$

$-5^{-2} = -\dfrac{1}{5^2}$ and $(-5)^{-2} = +\dfrac{1}{5^2}$

Example:

$2x^{-3} = \dfrac{2}{x^3}$

Simplify.

1) -6^{-1}

2) $-4x^{-3}$

3) $-\dfrac{5x}{x^{-3}}$

4) $-\dfrac{a^{-3}}{b^{-2}}$

5) $-\dfrac{5}{x^{-3}}$

6) $\dfrac{7b}{-9c^{-4}}$

7) $-\dfrac{5n^{-2}}{10p^{-3}}$

8) $\dfrac{4ab^{-2}}{-3c^{-2}}$

9) $-12x^2y^{-3}$

10) $(-\dfrac{1}{3})^{-2}$

11) $(-\dfrac{3}{4})^{-2}$

12) $(\dfrac{3a}{2c})^{-2}$

13) $(-\dfrac{5x}{3yz})^{-3}$

14) $-\dfrac{2x}{a^{-4}}$

Writing Scientific Notation

Helpful Hints

- It is used to write very big or very small numbers in decimal form.
- In scientific notation all numbers are written in the form of:

$$m \times 10^n$$

Decimal notation	Scientific notation
5	5×10^0
−25,000	$−2.5 \times 10^4$
0.5	5×10^{-1}
2,122.456	$2,122456 \times 10^3$

✏️ Write each number in scientific notation.

1) 91×10^3

2) 60

3) 2000000

4) 0.0000006

5) 354000

6) 0.000325

7) 2.5

8) 0.00023

9) 56000000

10) 2000000

11) 78000000

12) 0.0000022

13) 0.00012

14) 0.004

15) 78

16) 1600

17) 1450

18) 130000

19) 60

20) 0.113

21) 0.02

Square Roots

Helpful Hints
− A square root of x is a number r whose square is: $r^2 = x$

r is a square root of x.

Example:

$\sqrt{4} = 2$

✏️ Find the value each square root.

1) $\sqrt{1}$

2) $\sqrt{4}$

3) $\sqrt{9}$

4) $\sqrt{25}$

5) $\sqrt{16}$

6) $\sqrt{49}$

7) $\sqrt{36}$

8) $\sqrt{0}$

9) $\sqrt{64}$

10) $\sqrt{81}$

11) $\sqrt{121}$

12) $\sqrt{225}$

13) $\sqrt{144}$

14) $\sqrt{100}$

15) $\sqrt{256}$

16) $\sqrt{289}$

17) $\sqrt{324}$

18) $\sqrt{400}$

19) $\sqrt{900}$

20) $\sqrt{529}$

21) $\sqrt{90}$

Test Preparation

1) How is this number written in scientific notation?

    0.00002389

   A. 2.389×10^{-5}

   B. 23.89×10^{6}

   C. 0.2389×10^{-4}

   D. 2389×10^{-8}

2) How is this number written in scientific notation?

    0.000000502

   A. 5.02×10^{-7}

   B. 50.2×10^{8}

   C. 502×10^{-9}

   D. 0.502×10^{-6}

3) What is the product of the square root of 81 and the square root of 25?

   A. 2,025

   B. 15

   C. 25

   D. 45

4) Which of the following is equal to the square root of 72?

   A. $2\sqrt{6}$

   B. $36\sqrt{2}$

   C. $6\sqrt{2}$

   D. $12\sqrt{6}$

Answers of Worksheets – Chapter 11

Multiplication Property of Exponents

1) 4^4
2) 2^5
3) 3^4
4) $3x^4$
5) $36x^5$
6) $12x^3$
7) $25x^8$
8) $36x^5y^4$
9) $63x^3y^8$
10) $28x^4y^7$
11) $4x^4$
12) $24x^7y^6$
13) $560x^{11}y^4$
14) x^{12}
15) $16x^8$
16) x^6
17) $36x^2$
18) $21x^6y^8$

Division Property of Exponents

1) 5^4
2) $\frac{1}{3^4}$
3) $\frac{1}{2}$
4) 2^2
5) $\frac{1}{x^2}$
6) $\frac{1}{3x}$
7) $\frac{2}{9x^3}$
8) $3x^5$
9) $\frac{7}{4x}$
10) $\frac{3}{2x}$
11) $\frac{1}{2x^2}$
12) $\frac{3}{2x^2}$
13) $\frac{6}{7x^3}$
14) $\frac{4x^3}{3y^8}$
15) $\frac{5y^2}{x^5}$
16) $\frac{2x^3}{7}$
17) $\frac{4y^8}{x}$
18) $\frac{4}{5x^3y^9}$
19) $\frac{6}{5x^4}$
20) $\frac{16}{9x^4y}$
21) $\frac{1}{4}$

Powers of Products and Quotients

1) $16x^{12}$
2) $16x^2y^8$
3) $25x^8$
4) $121x^{10}$
5) $256x^8y^{16}$
6) $8x^{12}y^{12}$
7) $9x^4y^4$
8) $81x^{16}y^{12}$
9) $4x^{12}y^{16}$
10) $46,656x^6$
11) $8x^{45}$
12) $125x^{30}y^9$
13) $16x^{10}$
14) $225x^8$
15) $100x^{22}y^6$
16) $81x^{14}y^{10}$
17) $1,024x^{20}y^{30}$
18) $16x^8$

19) $144x^2y^6$ 20) $729x^6y^3$ 21) $144x^4y^{10}$

Zero and Negative Exponents

1) $\frac{1}{64}$
2) $\frac{1}{16}$
3) $\frac{1}{100}$
4) $\frac{1}{125}$
5) $\frac{1}{22}$
6) $\frac{1}{9}$
7) $\frac{1}{9}$
8) $\frac{1}{16}$
9) $\frac{1}{25}$
10) $\frac{1}{35}$
11) $\frac{1}{216}$
12) 0
13) $\frac{1}{1000000000}$
14) $\frac{1}{81}$
15) $\frac{1}{25}$
16) $\frac{1}{8}$
17) $\frac{1}{27}$
18) $\frac{1}{8}$
19) $\frac{1}{343}$
20) $\frac{1}{36}$
21) $\frac{9}{4}$
22) 125
23) 256
24) $\frac{125}{8}$

Negative Exponents and Negative Bases

1) $-\frac{1}{6}$
2) $-\frac{4}{x^3}$
3) $-5x^4$
4) $-\frac{b^2}{a^3}$
5) $-5x^3$
6) $-\frac{7bc^4}{9}$
7) $-\frac{p^3}{2n^2}$
8) $-\frac{4ac^2}{3b^2}$
9) $-\frac{12x^2}{y^3}$
10) 9
11) $\frac{16}{9}$
12) $\frac{4c^2}{9a^2}$
13) $-\frac{27y^3z^3}{125x^3}$
14) $-2xa^4$

Writing Scientific Notation

1) 9.1×10^4
2) 6×10^1
3) 2×10^6
4) 6×10^{-7}
5) 3.54×10^5
6) 3.25×10^{-4}
7) 2.5×10^0
8) 2.3×10^{-4}
9) 5.6×10^7
10) 2×10^6
11) 7.8×10^7
12) 2.2×10^{-6}

13) 1.2×10^{-4}
14) 4×10^{-3}
15) 7.8×10^{1}
16) 1.6×10^{3}
17) 1.45×10^{3}
18) 1.3×10^{5}
19) 6×10^{1}
20) 1.13×10^{-1}
21) 2×10^{-2}

Square Roots

1) 1
2) 2
3) 3
4) 5
5) 4
6) 7
7) 6
8) 0
9) 8
10) 9
11) 11
12) 15
13) 12
14) 10
15) 16
16) 17
17) 18
18) 20
19) 30
20) 23
21) $3\sqrt{10}$

Test Preparation Answers

1) Choice A is correct.

$0.00002389 = \frac{2.389}{100000} \Rightarrow 2.389 \times 10^{-5}$

2) Choice A is correct.

$0.000000502 = \frac{5.02}{10000000} \Rightarrow 5.02 \times 10^{-7}$

3) Choice D is correct.

4) Choice C is correct.

Chapter 12: Plane Figures

Topics that you'll learn in this chapter:

- ✓ Transformations: Translations, Rotations, and Reflections
- ✓ The Pythagorean Theorem
- ✓ Area of Triangles
- ✓ Perimeter of Polygons
- ✓ Area and Circumference of Circles
- ✓ Area of Squares, Rectangles, and Parallelograms
- ✓ Area of Trapezoids

Transformations: Translations, Rotations, and Reflections

Helpful Hints
- **Transformation:** A movement of a figure with certain properties.
- **Translation:** Moving every point in a shape in a specified direction.
- **Reflection:** The mirror image of a shape across an axis or a plane of reflection.
- **Rotation:** A transformation in a plane or a space that is the motion of a body around a fixed point.

✍ *Graph the image of the figure using the transformation given.*

1) translation: 4 units right and 1 unit down

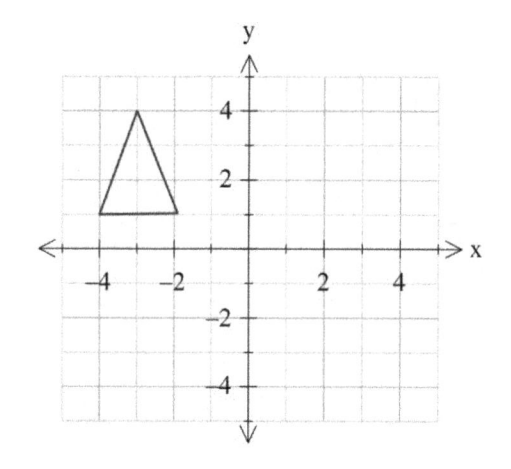

2) translation: 4 units right and 2 unit up

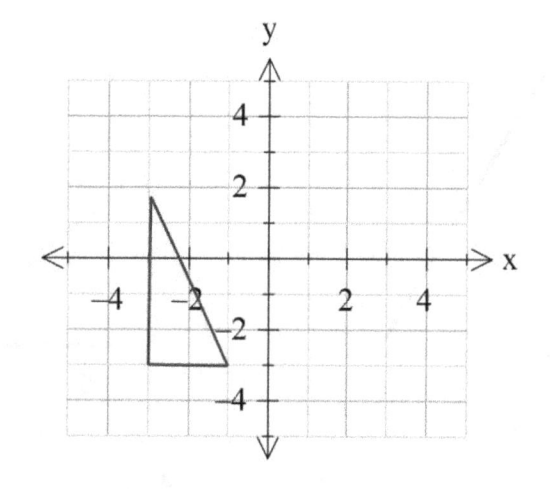

3) rotation 90° counterclockwise about the origin

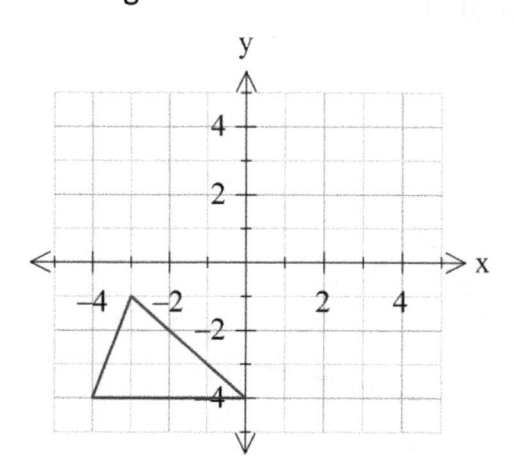

4) rotation 180° about the origin

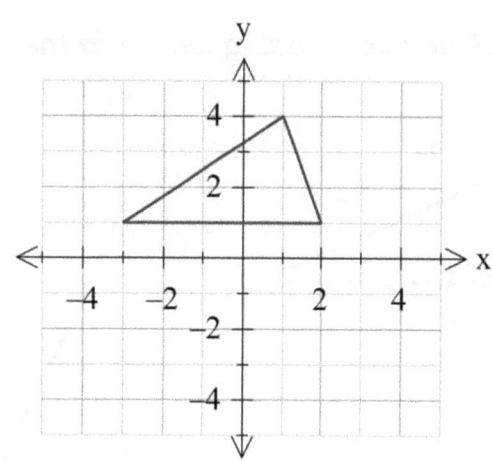

The Pythagorean Theorem

Helpful Hints

– In any right triangle:

$a^2 + b^2 = c^2$

Example:

Missing side = 5

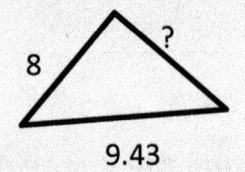

✎ **Do the following lengths form a right triangle?**

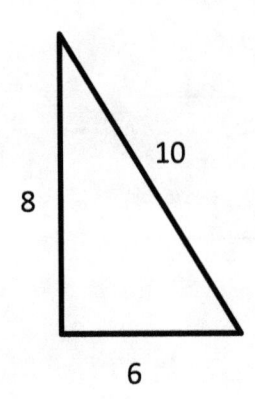

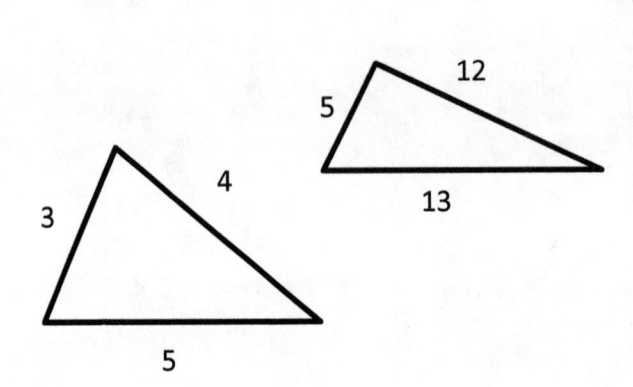

✎ **Find each missing length to the nearest tenth.**

4)

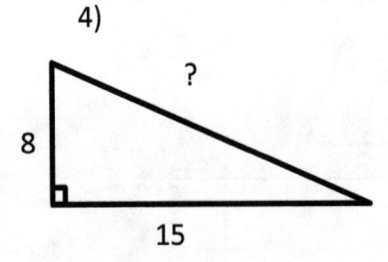

5)

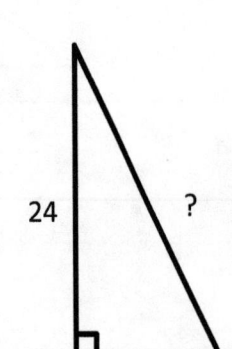

6)

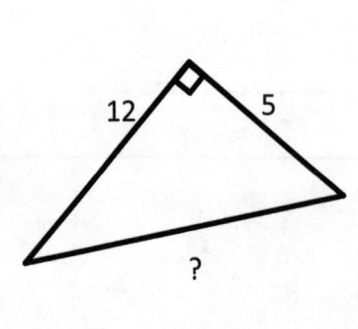

186

Area of Triangles

Helpful Hints

Area = $\frac{1}{2}$ (base × height)

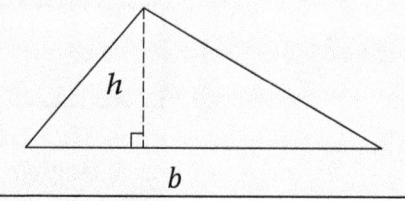

🖊 **Find the area of each.**

1) c = 9 mi

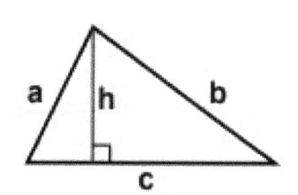

   h = 3.7 mi

2) s = 14 m

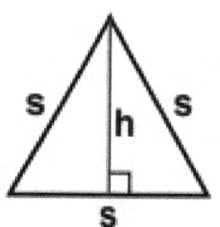

   h = 12.2 m

3) a = 5 m

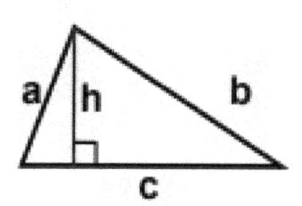

   b = 11 m

   c = 14 m

   h = 4 m

4) s = 10 m

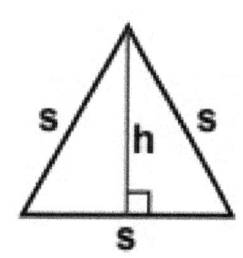

   h = 8.6 m

Perimeter of Polygons

Helpful Hints

Perimeter of a square = 4s

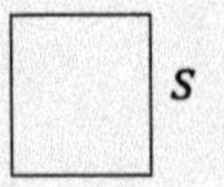

Perimeter of a rectangle = $2(l + w)$

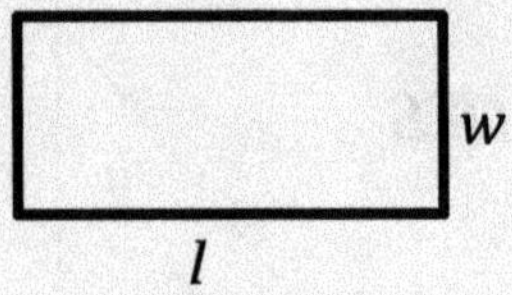

Perimeter of trapezoid = $a + b + c + d$

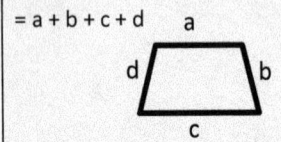

Perimeter of Pentagon = 6a

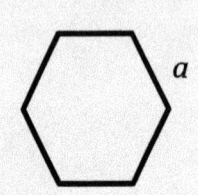

Perimeter of a parallelogram = $2(l + w)$

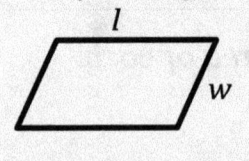

Example:

P = 18

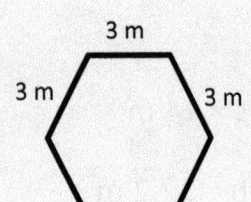

3 m, 3 m, 3 m

✎ **Find the perimeter of each shape.**

1) Hexagon with sides 5 m, 5 m, 5 m

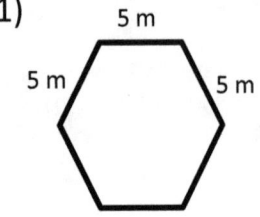

2) Parallelogram with sides 15 mm, 15 mm, 15 mm, 15mm

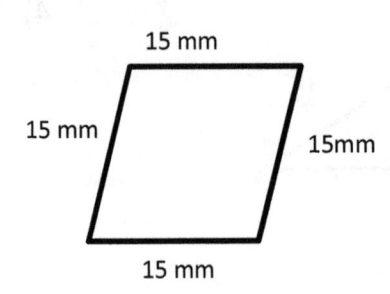

3) Rhombus with sides 12 ft, 12 ft, 12 ft, 12 ft

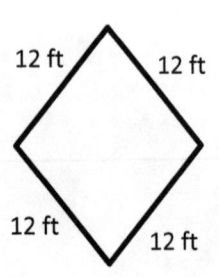

4) Rectangle 18 in by 12 in

188   www.EffortlessMath.com

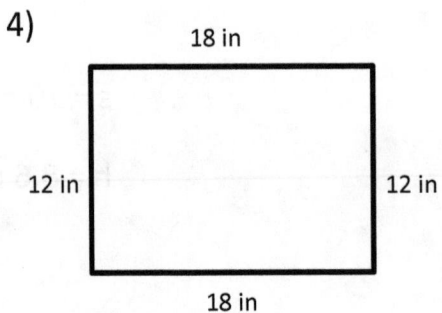

Area and Circumference of Circles

Helpful Hints

Area = πr²

Circumference = 2πr

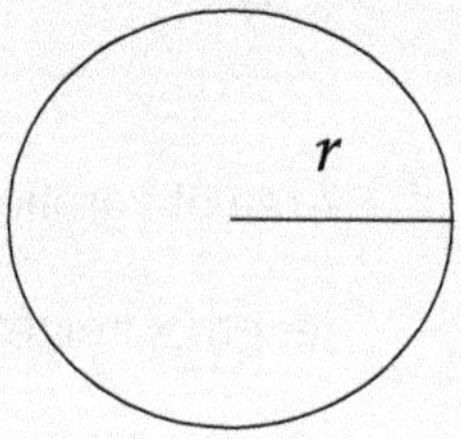

Example:

If the radius of a circle is 3, then:

Area = 28.27

Circumference = 18.85

✎ Find the area and circumference of each. (π = 3.14)

1) 4 in

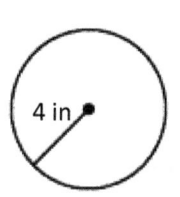

2) 18 cm

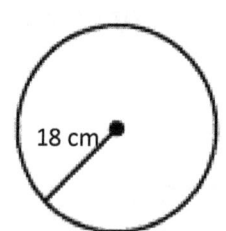

3) 5 m

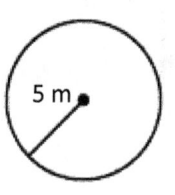

4) 11 cm

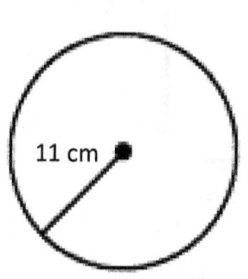

5) 8 km

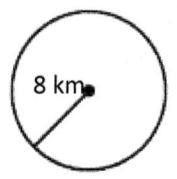

6) 21 in

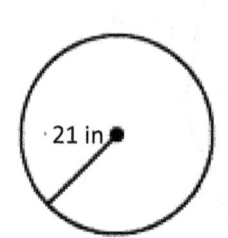

Area of Squares, Rectangles, and Parallelograms

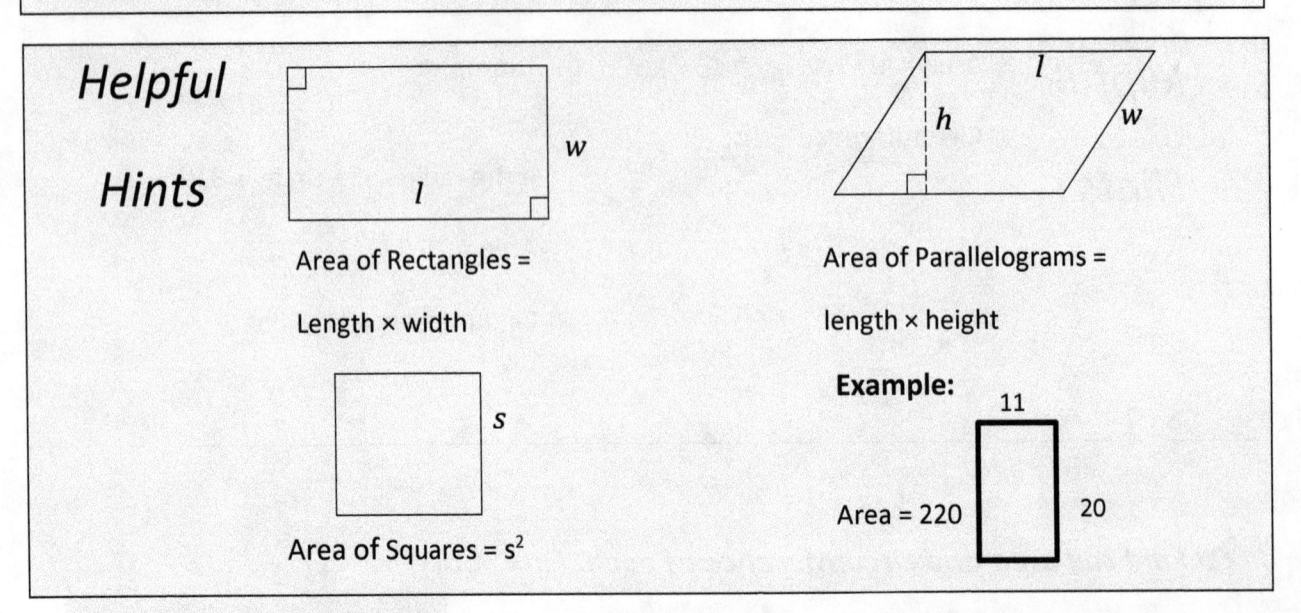

Helpful Hints

Area of Rectangles = Length × width

Area of Squares = s^2

Area of Parallelograms = length × height

Example:

Area = 220

✍ *Find the area of each.*

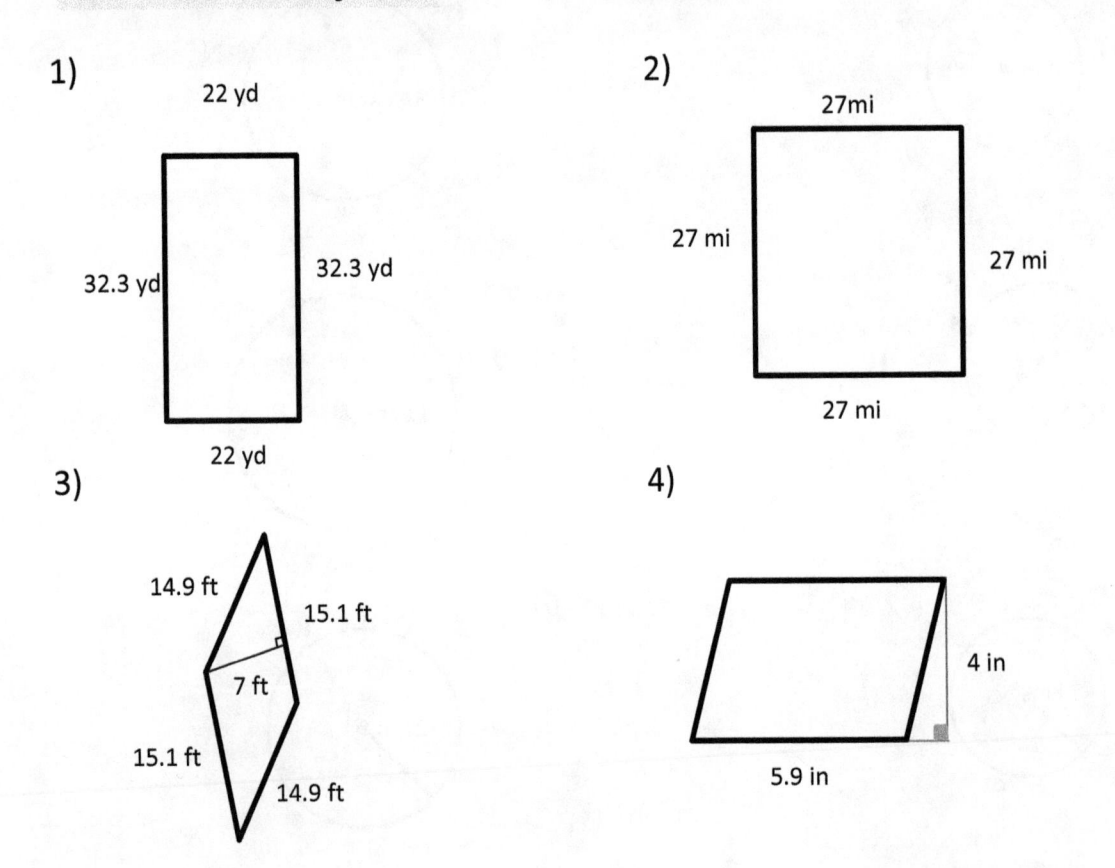

1) 22 yd, 32.3 yd, 32.3 yd, 22 yd

2) 27 mi, 27 mi, 27 mi, 27 mi

3) 14.9 ft, 15.1 ft, 7 ft, 15.1 ft, 14.9 ft

4) 4 in, 5.9 in

190

Area of Trapezoids

Helpful Hints

$A = \frac{1}{2} h(b_1 + b_2)$

Example:

$A = 252$ cm^2

16 cm
18 cm
12 cm

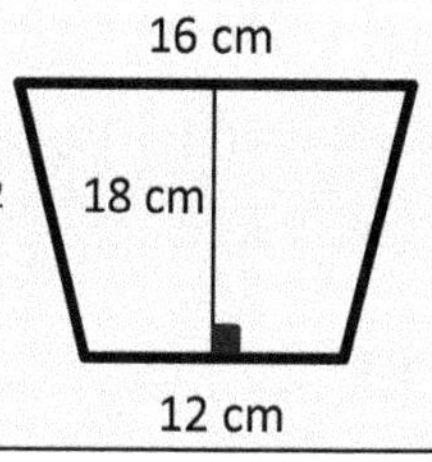

✎ Calculate the area for each trapezoid.

1)
9 cm
6 cm
12 cm

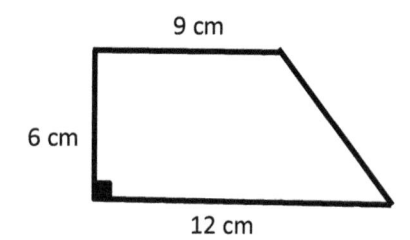

2)
14 m
10 m
18 m

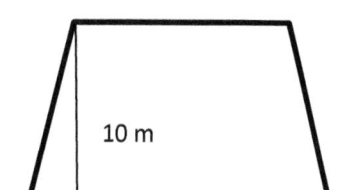

3)
22 mi
18 mi
20 mi
3 mi
22 mi

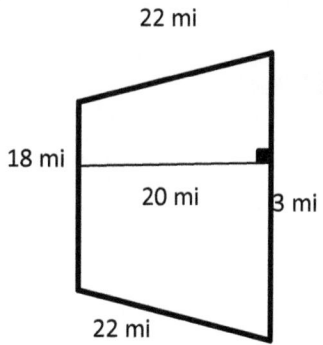

4)
8.6 nm
8.7 nm
7.8 nm
4.3 nm

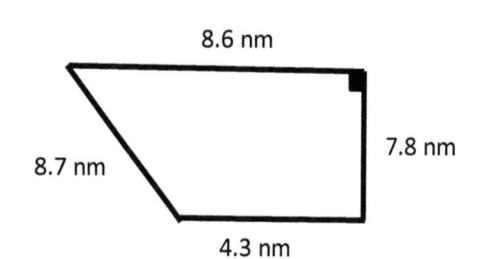

Test Preparation

1) A triangle is graphed on a coordinate grid and then reflected across the x–axis. If the center of the triangle was located at (x, y), which ordered pair represents the new center after the transformation?

   A. (x, y)

   B. $(x, -y)$

   C. $(-x, y)$

   D. $(-x, -y)$

2) The rectangle on the coordinate grid is translated 5 units down and 4 units to the left.

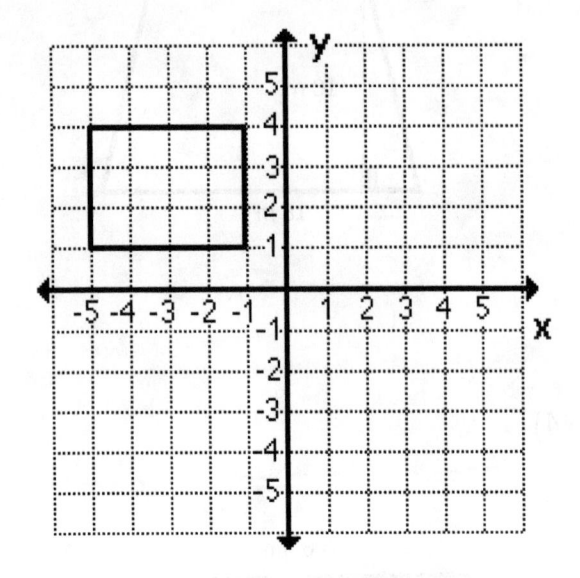

   Which of the following describes this transformation?

   A. $(x, y) \Rightarrow (x - 4, y + 5)$

   B. $(x, y) \Rightarrow (x - 4, y - 5)$

   C. $(x, y) \Rightarrow (x + 4, y + 5)$

   D. $(x, y) \Rightarrow (x + 4, y - 5)$

3) A circle is graphed on a coordinate grid and then reflected across the y–axis. If the center of the circle was located at (x, y), which ordered pair represents the new center after the transformation?

   A. (x, y)

   B. $(x, -y)$

   C. $(-x, y)$

   D. $(-x, -y)$

4) A boat sails 50 miles south and then 120 miles east. How far is the boat from its start point?

   A. 120 miles

   B. 130 miles

   C. 150 miles

   D. 170 miles

5) What is the estimated area of the shaded region?

   A. 11 cm²

   B. 42 cm²

   C. 153 cm²

   D. 196 cm²

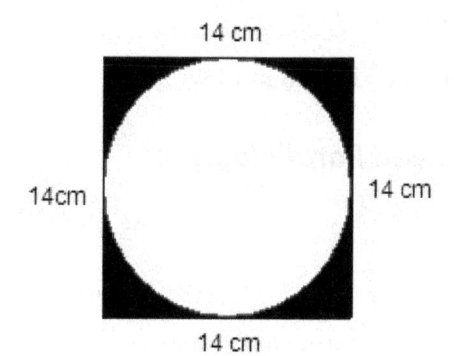

Answers of Worksheets – Chapter 12

The Pythagorean Theorem

1) yes
2) yes
3) yes
4) 17
5) 26
6) 13

Area of Triangles

1) 16.65 mi^2
2) 56 m^2
3) 85.4 m^2
4) 43 m^2

Perimeter of Polygons

1) 30 m
2) 60 mm
3) 48 ft
4) 60 in

Area and Circumference of Circles

1) Area: 50.24 in^2, Circumference: 25.12 in
2) Area: 1,017.36 cm^2, Circumference: 113.04 cm
3) Area: 78.5 m^2, Circumference: 31.4 m
4) Area: 379.94 cm^2, Circumference: 69.08 cm
5) Area: 200.96 km^2, Circumference: 50.2 km
6) Area: 1,384.74 km^2, Circumference: 131.88 km

Area of Squares, Rectangles, and Parallelograms

1) 710.6 yd^2
2) 729 mi^2
3) 105.7 ft^2
4) 23.6 in^2

Area of Trapezoids

1) 63 cm^2
2) 192 m^2
3) 451 mi^2
4) 50.31 nm^2

Test Preparation Answers

1) Choice B is correct.

When a point is reflected over x axes, the (y) coordinate of that point changes to $(-y)$, while its x coordinate remains the same.

2) Choice B is correct.

translated 5 units down and 4 units to the left means: $(x.y) \Rightarrow (x-4, y-5)$

3) Choice C is correct.

When a point is reflected over y axes, the (x) coordinate of that point changes to $(-x)$, while its y coordinate remains the same.

4) Choice B is correct.

Use the information provided in the question to draw the shape.

Use Pythagorean Theorem: $a^2 + b^2 = c^2$

$50^2 + 120^2 = c^2 \Rightarrow 2500 + 14400 = c^2 \Rightarrow 16900 = c^2 \Rightarrow c = 130$

5) Choice B is correct.

To estimate area of the shaded region, subtract area of the circle from area of the square.

The area of the square formula: $S = a^2$ and the area of circle formula: $S = \pi r^2$

Therefore, $S_{square} - S_{circle} = a^2 - \pi r^2 \Rightarrow S_{square} - S_{circle} = (14)^2 - \pi(\frac{14}{2})^2 \Rightarrow S_{square} - S_{circle} = 42 \text{ cm}^2$

Chapter 13: Solid Figures

Topics that you'll learn in this chapter:

- ✓ Volume of Cubes and Rectangle Prisms
- ✓ Surface Area of Cubes
- ✓ Surface Area of a Prism
- ✓ Volume of Pyramids and Cones
- ✓ Surface Area of Pyramids and Cones

Volume of Cubes and Rectangle Prisms

Helpful Hints
- Volume is the amount of space inside of a solid figure, like a rectangle prism, cube, or cylinder.
- Volume of a cube = (one side)³
- Volume of a rectangle prism: Length × Width × Height

✎ Find the volume of each of the rectangular prisms.

1) 14 cm, 12 cm, 8 cm

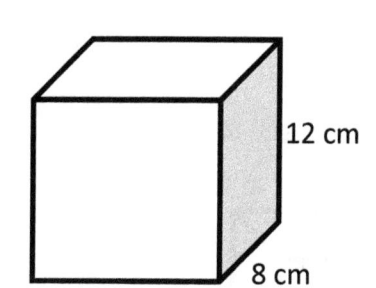

2) 22 cm, 15 cm, 11 cm, 5 cm

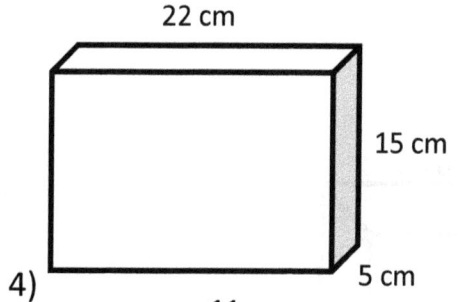

3) 8 m, 8 m, 8 m

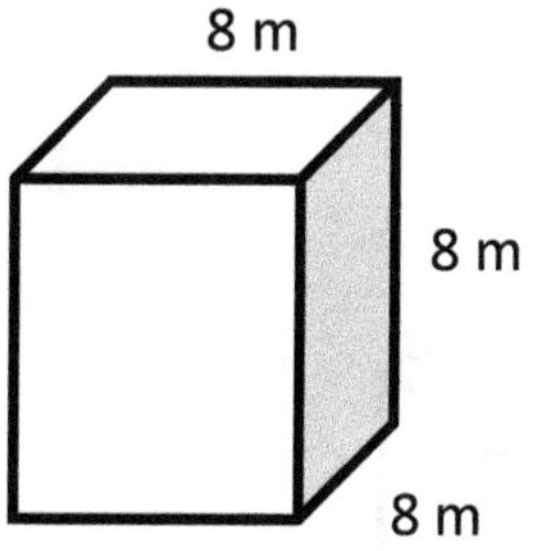

4) 13 cm, 8 cm

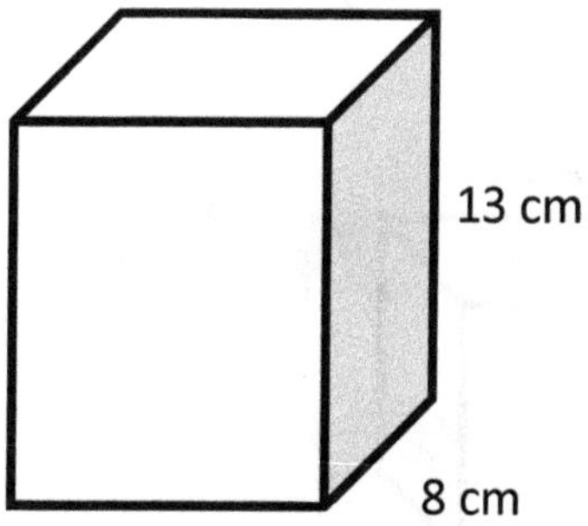

5)

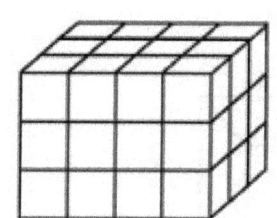

6)

---

www.EffortlessMath.com

197

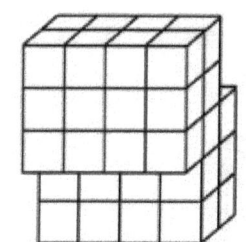

Surface Area of Cubes

Helpful Hints

Surface Area of a cube = $6 \times$ (one side of the cube)^2

Example:
$6 \times 4^2 = 96 m^3$

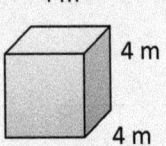

4 m
4 m
4 m

✎ *Find the surface of each cube.*

1)

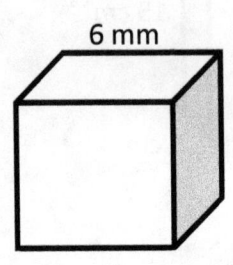

6 mm

2)

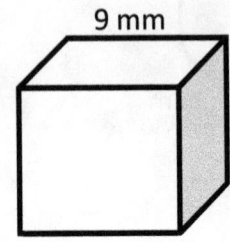

9 mm

3)

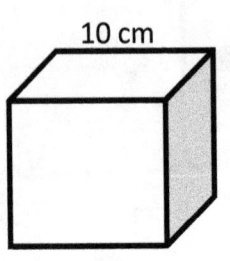

10 cm

4)

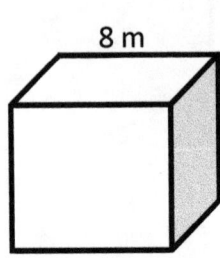

8 m

5)

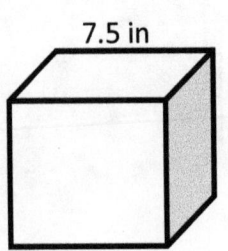

7.5 in

6)

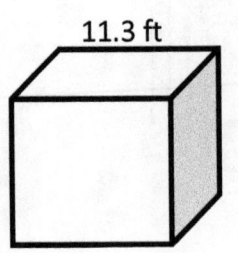

11.3 ft

198 www.EffortlessMath.com

Surface Area of a Prism

> *Helpful Hints*
>
> Surface Area of a Rectangle Prism Formula:
> SA =2 [(width × length) + (height × length) + width × height)]

🖎 *Find the surface of each prism.*

1)

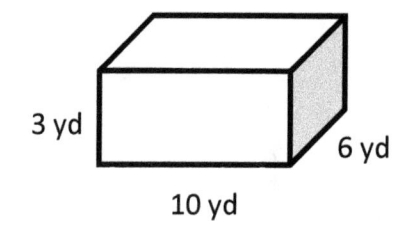

3 yd
6 yd
10 yd

2)

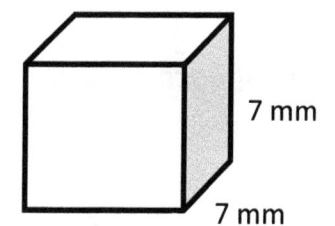

7 mm
7 mm

3)

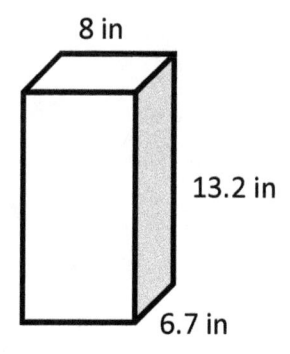

8 in
13.2 in
6.7 in

4)

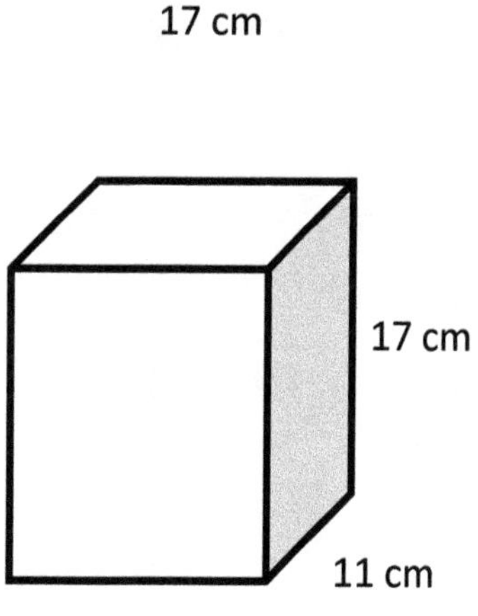

17 cm
17 cm
11 cm

FSA Mathematics Workbook For Grade 8

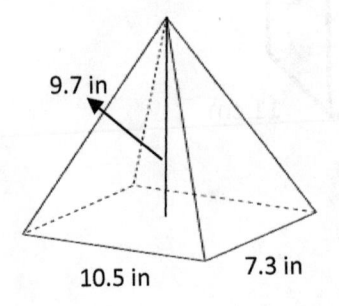

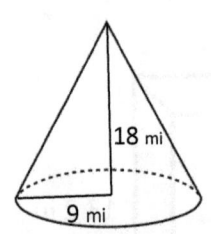

Volume of Pyramids and Cones

Helpful Hints

Volume of a pyramid $= \frac{1}{3} b \cdot h$

Volume of a cone $= \frac{1}{3} \pi r^2 h$

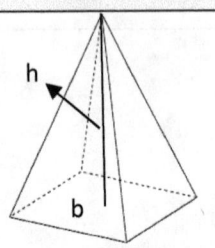

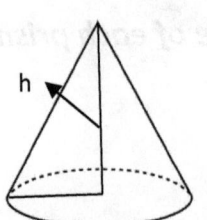

🖉 Find the volume of each figure.

1) cone: 14 yd (slant/height), 8 yd (radius)

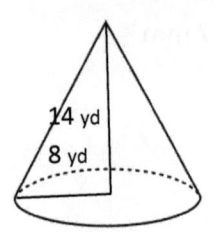

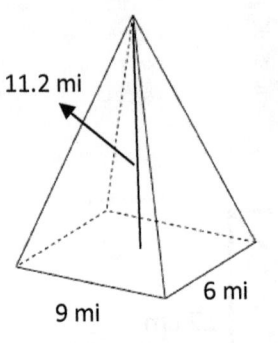

2) pyramid: 23 cm (height), 18 cm × 18 cm (base)

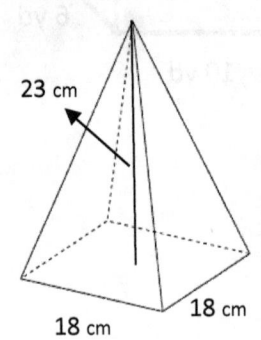

3) pyramid: 11.2 mi (height), 9 mi × 6 mi (base)

4) cone: 18 mi (height), 9 mi (radius)

5) pyramid: 9.7 in (height), 10.5 in × 7.3 in (base)

6) cone: 7 mi (height), 2 mi (radius)

200   www.EffortlessMath.com

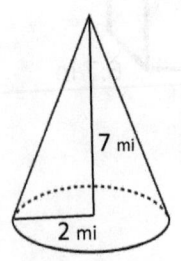

Surface Area of Pyramids and Cones

Helpful Hints

Surface Area Pyramid

$$lw + l\sqrt{(\frac{w}{2})^2 + h^2} + w\sqrt{(\frac{l}{2})^2 + h^2}$$

Surface Area Cone

$$= \pi r(r + \sqrt{h^2 + r^2})$$

✏️ Find the surface area of each figure.

1) Cone: 20 in (slant), 10 in (radius)

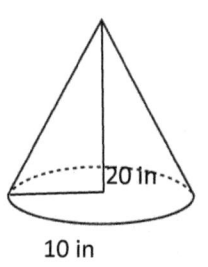

2) Pyramid: 22 in (slant height), 13 in × 13 in base

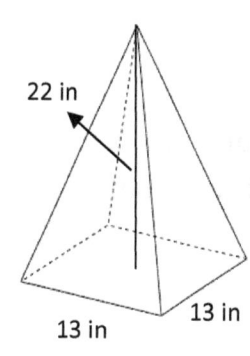

3) Pyramid: 19 m (slant height), 15 m × 15 m base

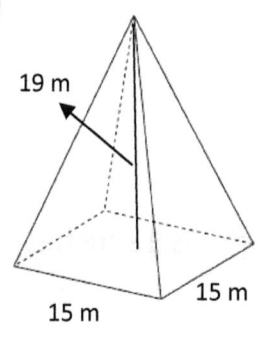

4) Cone: 25 cm (slant), 23 cm (radius)

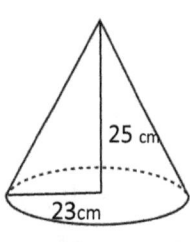

5) Pyramid: 15.4 ft (slant height), 18 ft × 18 ft base

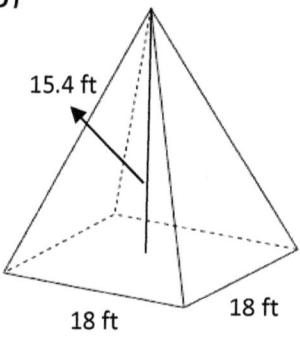

6) Cone: 24.7 km (slant), 11 km (radius)

www.EffortlessMath.com

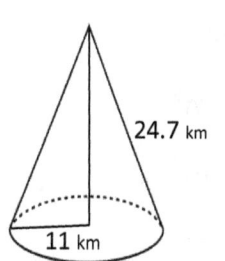

Test Preparation

1) What is the volume of the following square pyramid?

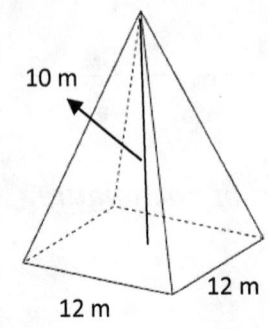

   A. 120 m³

   B. 144 m³

   C. 480 m³

   D. 1440 m³

   (10 m, 12 m, 12 m)

2) The width of a box is one third of its length. The height of the box is one third of its width. If the length of the box is 27 cm, what is the volume of the box?

   A. 81 cm³
   B. 162 cm³
   C. 243 cm³
   D. 729 cm³

3) The radius of the following cylinder is 8 inches and its height is 12 inches. What is the surface area of the cylinder?

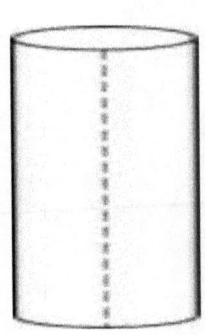

   A. 96 π cm²

   B. 192 π cm²

   C. 320 π cm²

   D. 768 π cm²

Answers of Worksheets – Chapter 13

Volume of Cubes and Rectangle Prisms

1) 1344 cm³
2) 1650 cm³
3) 512 m³
4) 1144 cm³
5) 36
6) 44

Surface Area of a Cube

1) 216 mm²
2) 486 mm²
3) 600 cm²
4) 384 m²
5) 337.5 in²
6) 766.14 ft²

Surface Area of a Prism

1) 216 yd²
2) 294 mm²
3) 495.28 in²
4) 1326 cm²
5) 126 in²
6) 14 cm²

Volume of Pyramids and Cones

1) 938.3 yd³
2) 2484 cm³
3) 201.6 mi³
4) 1526.8 mi³
5) 247.835 in³
6) 29.3 mi³

Surface Area of Pyramids and Cones

1) 942.48 in³
2) 596.444 in²
3) 612.8 m³
4) 468.32 m³
5) 642.1334 ft²
6) 233.7 km²

Test Preparation Answers

1) Choice C is correct

Use the volume of square pyramid formula.

$V = \frac{1}{3}a^2h \Rightarrow V = \frac{1}{3}(12m)^2 \times 10m \Rightarrow V = 480 \, m^3$

2) Choice D is correct

If the length of the box is 27, then the width of the box is one third of it, 9, and the height of the box is 3 (one third of the width). The volume of the box is:

$V = (length)(width)(height) = (27)(9)(3) = 729 \, m^3$

3) Choice C is correct.

Cylinder surface Area = Areas of top and bottom + Area of the side

Surface Area = 2(Area of top) + (perimeter of top) × height

Surface Area = $2(\pi r^2) + (2\pi r) \times h$

Surface Area = $2(\pi 8^2) + (2\pi \times 8) \times 12 \Rightarrow$ Surface Area = $128\pi + 192\pi \Rightarrow$ Surface Area = 320π

Chapter 14: Statistics

Topics that you'll learn in this chapter:

- ✓ Mean, Median, Mode, and Range of the Given Data
- ✓ First Quartile, Second Quartile and Third Quartile of the Given Data
- ✓ Bar Graph
- ✓ Box and Whisker Plots
- ✓ Stem–And–Leaf Plot
- ✓ The Pie Graph or Circle Graph
- ✓ Scatter Plots

Mean, Median, Mode, and Range of the Given Data

Helpful Hints

- Mean: $\dfrac{\text{sum of the data}}{\text{of data entires}}$
- Mode: value in the list that appears most often
- Range: largest value – smallest value

Example:

22, 16, 12, 9, 7, 6, 4, 6

Mean = 10.25

Mod = 6

Range = 18

✏️ Find Mean, Median, Mode, and Range of the Given Data.

1) 7, 2, 5, 1, 1, 2

2) 2, 2, 2, 3, 6, 3, 7, 4

3) 9, 4, 3, 1, 7, 9, 4, 6, 4

4) 8, 4, 2, 4, 3, 2, 4, 5

5) 8, 5, 7, 5, 7, 9, 8

6) 5, 1, 4, 4, 9, 2, 9, 2, 5, 1

7) 4, 1, 5, 9, 7, 7, 5, 4, 3, 5

8) 7, 5, 4, 9, 6, 7, 7, 5, 2

9) 2, 5, 5, 6, 2, 4, 7, 6, 4, 9

10) 10, 5, 2, 5, 4, 5, 8, 10

11) 5, 1, 5, 2, 2

12) 2, 3, 5, 9, 6

First Quartile, Second Quartile and Third Quartile of the Given Data

Helpful Hints

Quartile 1: It's the number halfway from smallest number and the median of the data set.

Quartile 2: It's the median and cuts data set in half.

Quartile 3: It's the number halfway from the median and the biggest number of the data set.

✍ *Find First Quartile, Second Quartile and Third Quartile of the Given Data.*

1) 65, 8, 35, 54, 29, 42, 14, 73, 11

2) 14, 64, 30, 20, 72, 57

3) 99, 37, 83, 62, 74, 49, 59, 40

4) 33, 14, 47, 29, 52, 63, 20, 39, 74, 48

5) 23, 10, 13, 30, 26, 8, 25, 18

6) 35, 60, 20, 80, 95, 15, 40, 85, 75

Box and Whisker Plots

> *Helpful Hints*
>
> Box–and–whisker plots display data including quartiles.
> - IQR – interquartile range shows the difference from Q1 to Q3.
> - Extreme Values are the smallest and largest values in a data set.

Example:

73, 84, 86, 95, 68, 67, 100, 94, 77, 80, 62, 79

Maximum: 100, Minimum: 62, Q_1: 70.5, Q_2: 79.5, Q_3: 90

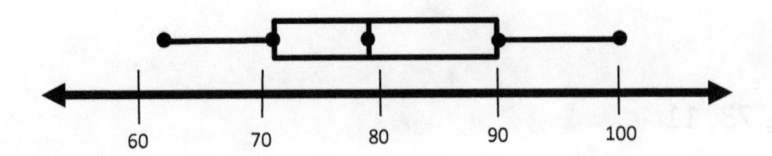

✎ **Make box and whisker plots for the given data.**

11, 17, 22, 18, 23, 2, 3, 16, 21, 7, 8, 15, 5

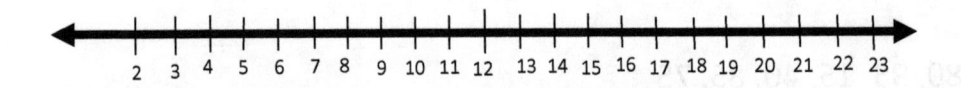

208

Bar Graph

Helpful Hints — A bar graph is a chart that presents data with bars in different heights to match with the values of the data. The bars can be graphed horizontally or vertically.

✎ *Graph the given information as a bar graph.*

Day	Hot dogs sold
Monday	90
Tuesday	70
Wednesday	30
Thursday	20
Friday	60

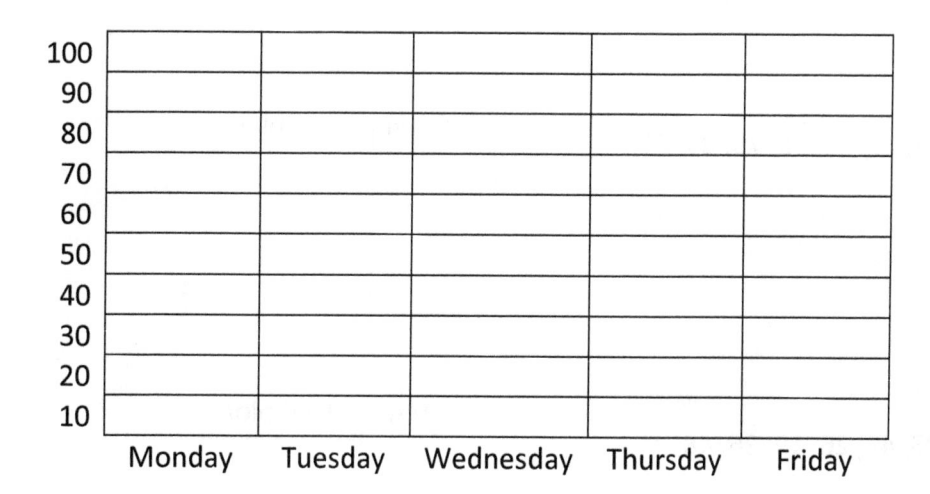

Stem–And–Leaf Plot

Helpful Hints
— Stem–and–leaf plots display the frequency of the values in a data set.
— We can make a frequency distribution table for the values, or we can use a stem–and–leaf plot.

Example:

56, 58, 42, 48, 66, 64, 53, 69, 45, 72

Stem	leaf
4	2 5 8
5	3 6 8
6	4 6 9
7	2

✎ *Make stem ad leaf plots for the given data.*

1) 74, 88, 97, 72, 79, 86, 95, 79, 83, 91

   Stem | Leaf plot

2) 37, 48, 26, 33, 49, 26, 19, 26, 48

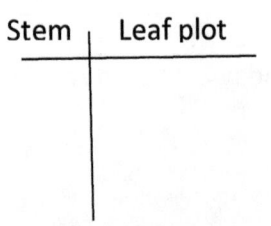

   Stem | Leaf plot

3) 58, 41, 42, 67, 54, 65, 65, 54, 69, 53

   Stem | Leaf plot

The Pie Graph or Circle Graph

Helpful Hints

A Pie Chart is a circle chart divided into sectors, each sector represents the relative size of each value.

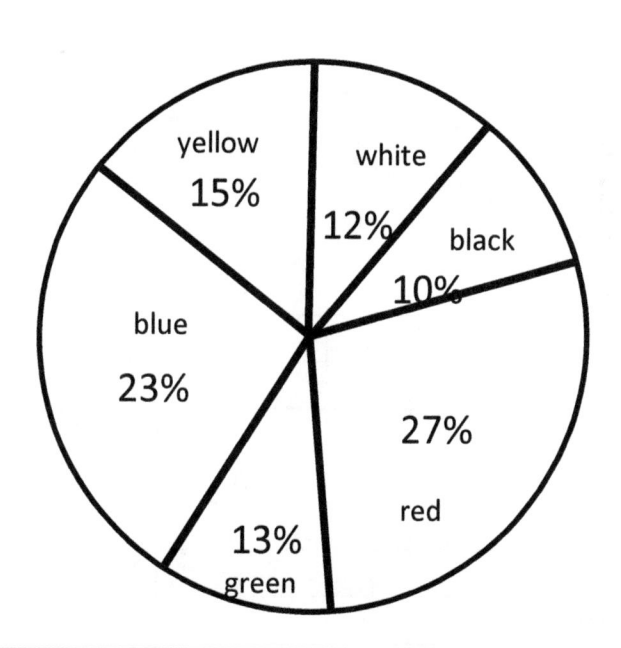

Pie chart data:
- yellow 15%
- white 12%
- black 10%
- red 27%
- green 13%
- blue 23%

Favorite colors

1) Which color is the most?

2) What percentage of pie graph is yellow?

3) Which color is the least?

4) What percentage of pie graph is blue?

5) What percentage of pie graph is green?

Scatter Plots

Helpful Hints

A Scatter (xy) Plot shows the values with points that represent the relationship between two sets of data.

— The horizontal values are usually x and vertical data is y.

✎ Construct a scatter plot.

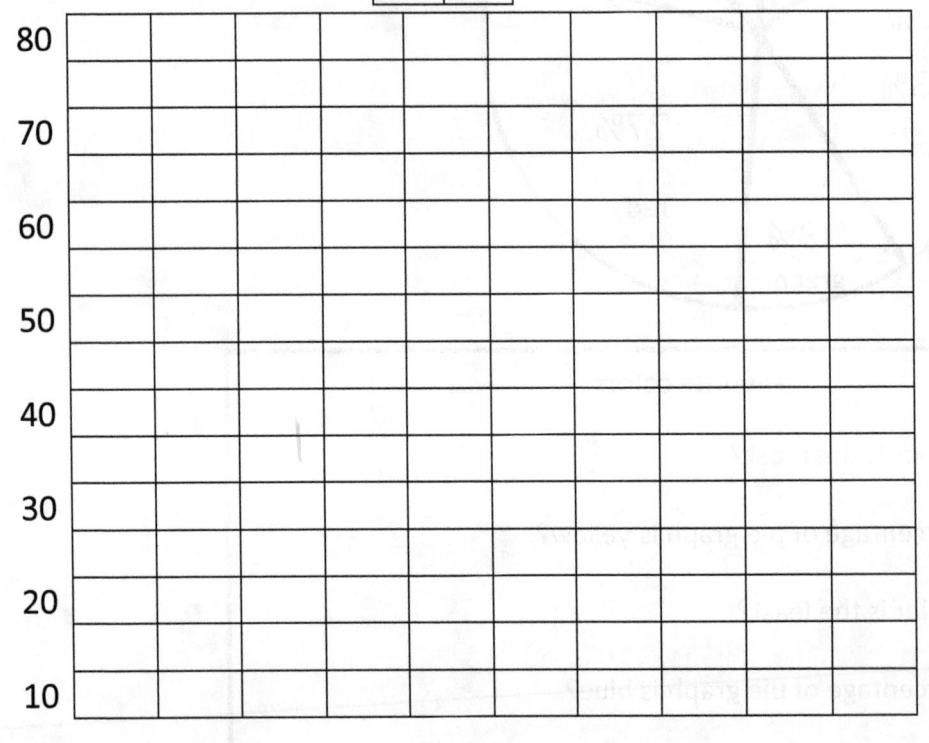

X	Y
1	20
2	40
3	50
4	60

Test Preparation

1) What is the median of these numbers? 33, 18, 12, 77, 19, 44, 2

   A. 33
   B. 18
   C. 19
   D. 77

2) What is the median of these numbers? 2, 22, 28, 19, 67, 44, 35

   A. 19
   B. 28
   C. 44
   D. 35

3) The following graph shows the mark of six students in mathematics. What is the mean (average) of the marks?

   A. 15
   B. 14.5
   C. 14
   D. 13.5

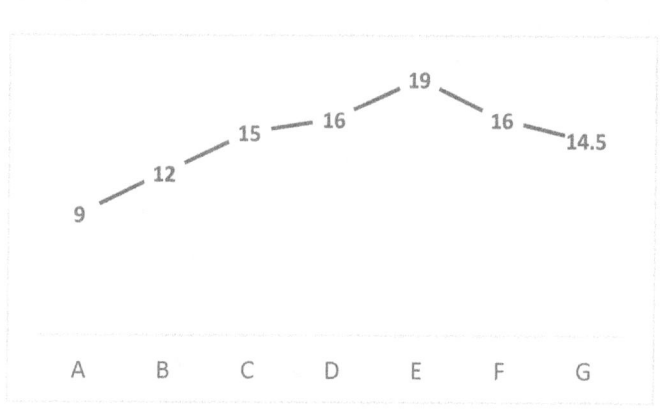

4) In the following graph, which of the data point is farthest from the line of best fit (not shown)?

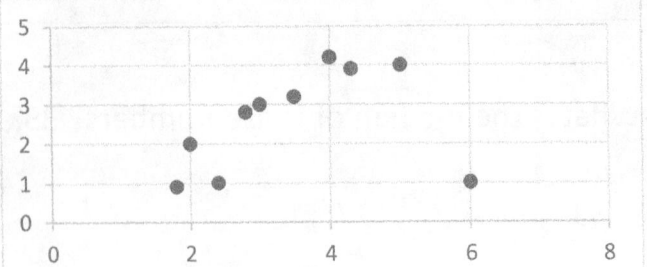

   A. (6, 1)
   B. (5, 4)
   C. (3, 3)
   D. (2, 2)

5) The circle graph below shows all Mr. Green's expenses for last month. If he spent $660 on his car, how much did he spend for his rent?

   A. $700
   B. $740
   C. $780
   D. $810

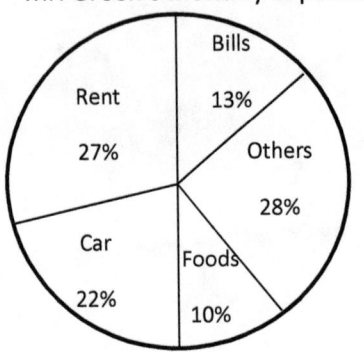

Mr. Green's monthly expenses
- Rent 27%
- Bills 13%
- Others 28%
- Foods 10%
- Car 22%

Answers of Worksheets – Chapter 14

Mean, Median, Mode, and Range of the Given Data

1) mean: 3, median: 2, mode: 1, 2, range: 6
2) mean: 3.625, median: 3, mode: 2, range: 5
3) mean: 5.22, median: 4, mode: 4, range: 8
4) mean: 4, median: 4, mode: 4, range: 6
5) mean: 7, median: 7, mode: 5, 7, 8, range: 4
6) mean: 4.2, median: 4, mode: 1,2,4,5,9, range: 8
7) mean: 5, median: 5, mode: 5, range: 8
8) mean: 5.78, median: 6, mode: 7, range: 7
9) mean: 5, median: 5, mode: 2, 4, 5, 6, range: 7
10) mean: 6.125, median: 5, mode: 5, range: 8
11) mean: 3, median: 2, mode: 2, 5, range: 4
12) mean: 5, median: 5, mode: none, range: 7

First Quartile, Second Quartile and Third Quartile of the Given Data

1) First quartile: 12.5, second quartile: 35, third quartile: 59.5
2) First quartile: 20, second quartile: 43.5, third quartile: 64
3) First quartile: 44.5, second quartile: 60.5, third quartile: 78.5
4) First quartile: 29, second quartile: 43, third quartile: 52
5) First quartile: 11.5, second quartile: 20.5, third quartile: 25.5
6) First quartile: 27.5, second quartile: 60, third quartile: 82.5

Box and Whisker Plots

11, 17, 22, 18, 23, 2, 3, 16, 21, 7, 8, 15, 5

Maximum: 23, Minimum: 2, Q_1: 2, Q_2: 12.5, Q_3: 19.5

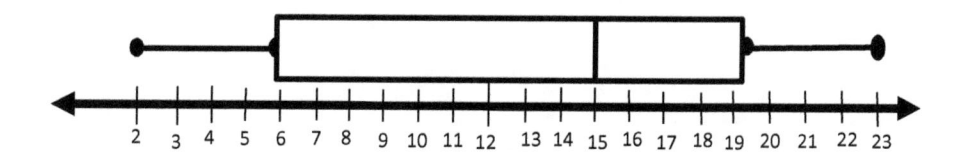

Bar Graph

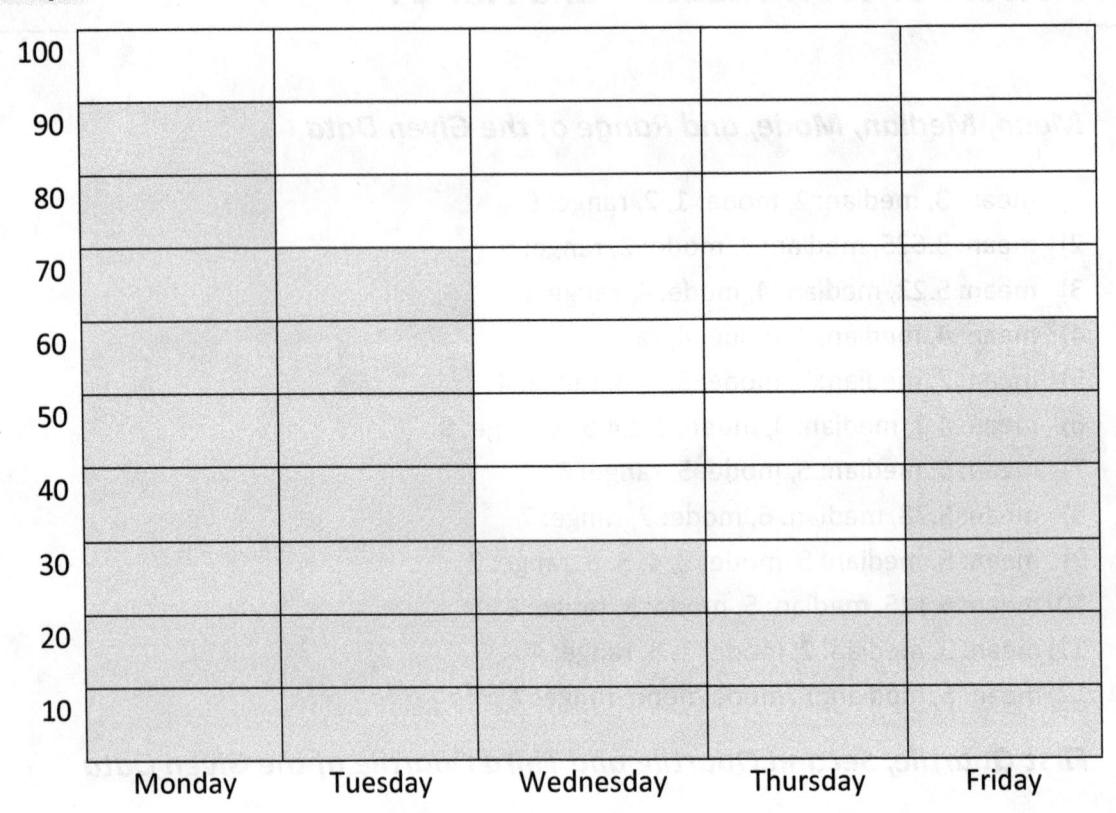

Stem–And–Leaf Plot

1)

Stem	leaf
7	2 4 9 9
8	3 6 8
9	1 5 7

2)

Stem	leaf
1	9
2	6 6 6
3	3 7
4	8 8 9

3)

Stem	leaf
4	1 2
5	3 4 4 8
6	5 5 7 9

The Pie Graph or Circle Graph

1) red
2) 15%
3) black
4) 23%
5) 13%

Scatter Plots

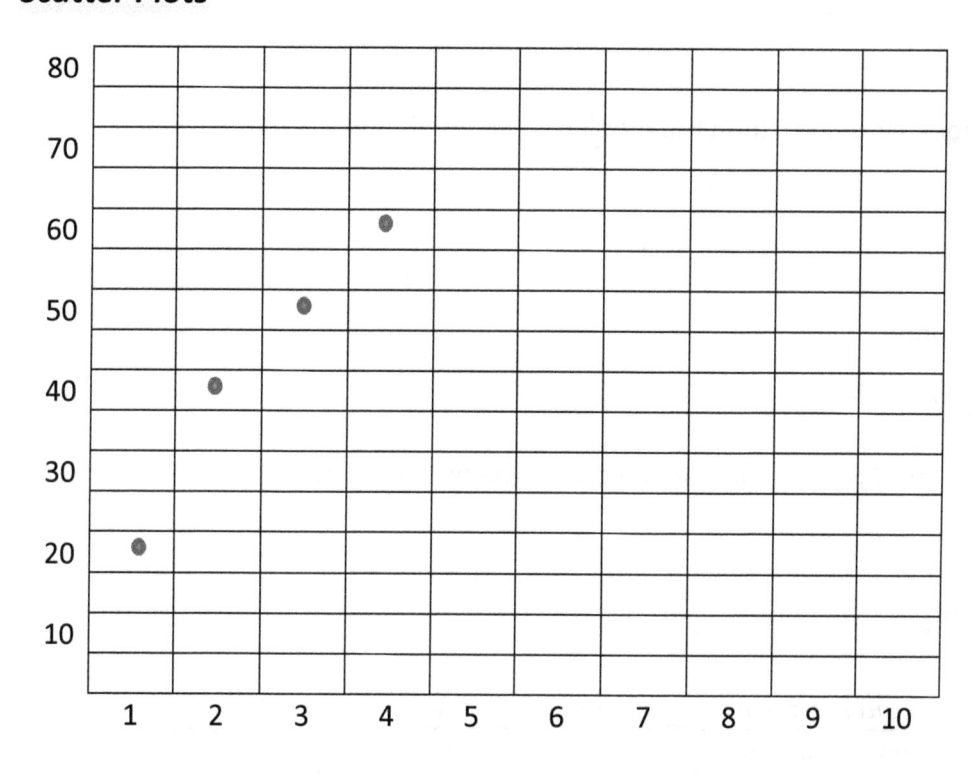

Test Preparation Answers

1) Choice C is correct.

Write the numbers in order:

2, 12, 18, 19, 33, 44, 77

Since we have 7 numbers (7 is odd), then the median is the number in the middle, which is 19.

2) Choice B is correct.

Write the numbers in order:

2, 19, 22, 28, 35, 44, 67

Since we have 7 numbers (7 is odd), then the median is the number in the middle, which is 28.

3) Choice B is correct

$$average\ (mean) = \frac{sum\ of\ terms}{number\ of\ terms} = \frac{9 + 12 + 15 + 16 + 19 + 16 + 14.5}{7} = 14.5$$

4) Choice A is correct

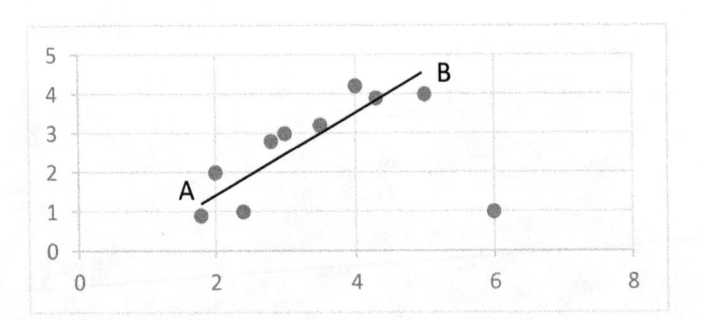

Line AB is the best fit line.

Then, point (6, 1) is the farthest from line AB.

5) Choice D is correct

Let x be all expenses, then $\frac{22}{100}x = \$660 \rightarrow x = \frac{100 \times \$660}{22} = \$3000$

He spent for his rent: $\frac{27}{100} \times \$3000 = \$810$

Chapter 15: Probability

Topics that you'll learn in this chapter:

- ✓ Probability of Simple Events
- ✓ Experimental Probability
- ✓ Independent and Dependent Events Word Problems
- ✓ Factorials
- ✓ Permutations
- ✓ Combination

Probability of Simple Events

> ***Helpful Hints***
>
> - Probability is the likelihood of something happening in the future. It is expressed as a number between zero (can never happen) to 1 (will always happen).
> - Probability can be expressed as a fraction, a decimal, or a percent.
>
> **Example:**
> Probability of a flipped coins turns up 'heads'
> Is $0.5 = \frac{1}{2}$

✎ *Solve.*

1) A number is chosen at random from 1 to 10. Find the probability of selecting a 4 or smaller.

2) A number is chosen at random from 1 to 50. Find the probability of selecting multiples of 10.

3) A number is chosen at random from 1 to 10. Find the probability of selecting of 4 and factors of 6.

4) A number is chosen at random from 1 to 10. Find the probability of selecting a multiple of 3.

5) A number is chosen at random from 1 to 50. Find the probability of selecting prime numbers.

6) A number is chosen at random from 1 to 25. Find the probability of not selecting a composite number.

Experimental Probability

> **Helpful Hints** — Experimental probability refers to the probability of an event occurring when an experiment was conducted.
>
> Experimental probability = $\dfrac{\text{Number of event occurrences}}{\text{Total number of trials}}$

On cube	frequency
1	6
2	7
3	8
4	5
5	4

1) What is the theoretical probability for rolling a number greater than 3?

2) What was the experimental probability of rolling a number greater than 4?

3) Is there any difference between theoretical and experimental probability?

4) How many times did you actually roll the number one in the experiment?

5) Theoretically if you roll a number cube 36 times, how many times would you expect to roll the number one?

Factorials

> *Helpful Hints*
>
> Means to multiply a series of descending natural numbers.
>
> Example:
>
> $4! = 4 \times 3 \times 2 \times 1$

✎ **Determine the value for each expression.**

1) $\dfrac{9!}{6!}$

2) $\dfrac{8!}{5!}$

3) $\dfrac{7!}{5!}$

4) $\dfrac{20!}{18!}$

5) $\dfrac{22!}{18!5!}$

6) $\dfrac{10!}{8!2!}$

7) $\dfrac{100!}{97!}$

8) $\dfrac{14!}{10!4!}$

9) $\dfrac{10!}{8!}$

10) $\dfrac{25!}{20!}$

11) $\dfrac{14!}{9!3!}$

12) $\dfrac{55!}{53!}$

13) $\dfrac{(2 \cdot 3)!}{3!}$

14) $5! + 4!$

Permutations

Helpful Hints

The number of ways to choose a sample of r elements from a set of n distinct objects where order does matter and replacements are not allowed.

$$_nP_k = \frac{n!}{(n-k)!}$$

Example:

$$_4P_2 = \frac{4!}{(4-2)!}$$
$$= 12$$

✏️ *Evaluate each expression.*

1) $_4P_2$

2) $_5P_1$

3) $_6P_2$

4) $_6P_6$

5) $-4 + {_7P_4}$

6) $5 \cdot {_6P_5}$

7) $_7P_2$

8) $_4P_1$

9) $_8P_5$

10) $_7P_3$

11) How many possible 7–digit telephone numbers are there? Someone left their umbrella on the subway and we need to track them down.

12) With repetition allowed, how many ways can one choose 8 out of 12 things?

Combination

Helpful Hints

The number of ways to choose a sample of r elements from a set of n distinct objects where order does not matter and replacements are not allowed.

$_nC_r = \dfrac{n!}{r!\,(n-r)!}$

Example:

$_4C_2 = \dfrac{4!}{2!(4-2)!}$

$= 3$

✎ List all possible combinations.

1) 4, 5, 6, 7, taken four at a time

2) T, V, W, taken two at a time

✎ Evaluate each expression.

3) $_7C_5$

4) $_4C_2$

5) $_9C_3$

6) $_5C_2$

7) $_{12}C_8$

8) $_9C_6$

9) $_{22}C_{20}$

10) $_{12}C_8$

11) $_{11}C_8$

12) $_{25}C_{23}$

13) $_{17}C_{10}$

14) $_{24}C_5$

15) $4 \cdot {_{18}C_{11}}$

16) $_{20}C_{16} + 1$

Test Preparation

1) A bag contains 18 balls: two green, five black, eight blue, a brown, a red and one white. If 17 balls are removed from the bag at random, what is the probability that a brown ball has been removed?

   A. $\frac{1}{9}$

   B. $\frac{1}{6}$

   C. $\frac{16}{17}$

   D. $\frac{17}{18}$

2) How many possible outfit combinations come from six shirts, three slacks, and five ties?

   Write your answer in the box below.

6) Two dice are thrown simultaneously, what is the probability of getting a sum of 6 or 9?

   A. $\frac{1}{3}$

   B. $\frac{1}{4}$

   C. $\frac{1}{6}$

   D. $\frac{1}{12}$

Answers of Worksheets – Chapter 15

Probability of simple events

1) $\frac{1}{6}$ 2) $\frac{1}{3}$

3) {(3, 3), (3, 5), (3, 7), (5, 3), (5, 5), (5, 7), (7, 3), (7, 5), (7, 7)}
4) {(T, 3), (T, 4), (T, 5), (W, 3), (W, 4), (W, 5), (R, 3), (R, 4), (R, 5)}
5) {Tuesday, Wednesday, Thursday}
6) {ham, turkey, chicken}
7) {(B_1, B_2), (B_1, G), (B_2, B_1), (B_2, G), (G, B_1), (G, B_2)}

Experimental Probability

1) 1/3   2) 2/15   3) yes   4) 6   5) 6

Factorials

1) 504   6) 45   11) 40,040
2) 336   7) 970,200   12) 2,970
3) 42   8) 1,001   13) 120
4) 380   9) 90   14) 144
5) 1,463   10) 6,375,600

Permutations

1) 12
2) 5
3) 30
4) 720
5) 836
6) 3,600
7) 42
8) 4
9) 6,720
10) 210
13) 10^7
14) 12^8

Combination

1) 4567
2) TV VW TW
3) 27
4) 6
5) 84
6) 10
7) 495
8) 84
9) 231
10) 495
11) 165
12) 300
13) 19,448
14) 42,504
15) 127,296
16) 4,846
17) 11,622

Test Preparation Answers

1) Choice D is correct

If 17 balls are removed from the bag at random, there will be one ball in the bag.

The probability of choosing a brown ball is 1 out of 18. Therefore, the probability of not choosing a brown ball is 17 out of 18 and the probability of having not a brown ball after removing 17 balls is the same.

2) The answer is 90.

To find the number of possible outfit combinations, multiply number of options for each factor:

6 × 3 × 5 = 90

3) Choice B is correct

For sum of 6: (1 & 5) and (5 & 1), (2 & 4) and (4 & 2), (3 & 3), therefore we have 5 options.

For sum of 9: (3 & 6) and (6 & 3), (4 & 5) and (5 & 4), we have 4 options.

To get a sum of 6 or 9 for two dice: 5 + 4 = 9

Since, we have 6 × 6 = 36 total number of options, the probability of getting a sum of 6 and 9 is 9 out of 36 or $\frac{9}{36} = \frac{1}{4}$.

FSA Mathematics Practice Tests

FSA Mathematics
Practice Test 1

The Florida Standards Assessments

Grade 8

Mathematics

2019

Grade 8 FSA Mathematics Reference Sheet

Customary Conversions

1 foot = 12 inches

1 yard = 3 feet

1 mile = 5,280 feet

1 mile = 1,760 yards

1 cup = 8 fluid ounces

1 pint = 2 cups

1 quart = 2 pints

1 gallon = 4 quarts

1 pound = 16 ounces

1 ton = 2,000 pounds

Metric Conversions

1 meter = 100 centimeters

1 meter = 1000 millimeters

1 kilometer = 1000 meters

1 liter = 1000 milliliters

1 gram = 1000 milligrams

1 kilogram = 1000 grams

Time Conversions

1 minute = 60 seconds

1 hour = 60 minutes

1 day = 24 hours

1 year = 365 days

1 year = 52 weeks

Formulas

Area of parallelogram =

base × height

Area of Rectangle =

Length × Width

Volume = base × height

Volume of pyramid = $\frac{1}{3}$ Bh

Scientific Calculators are NOT permitted for Session 1.

Time for Session 1: 60 Minutes

Session 1

1) A rope weighs 600 grams per meter of length. What is the weight in kilograms of 12.2 meters of this rope? (1 kilograms = 1000 grams)
   A. 0.0732
   B. 0.732
   C. 7.32
   D. 7,320

2) In a school, the ratio of number of boys to girls is 3:7. If the number of boys is 180, what is the total number of students in the school?
   Write your answer in the box below.

   ☐

3) In two successive years, the population of a town is increased by 15% and 20%. What percent of its population is increased after two years?
   A. 32
   B. 35
   C. 38
   D. 68

4) Which graph shows a non–proportional linear relationship between x and y?

A.

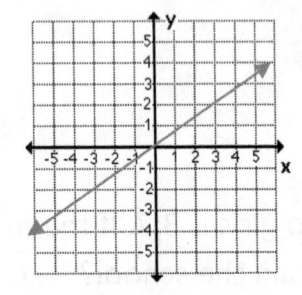

B.

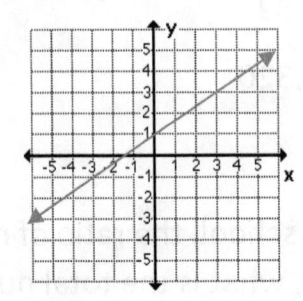

C.

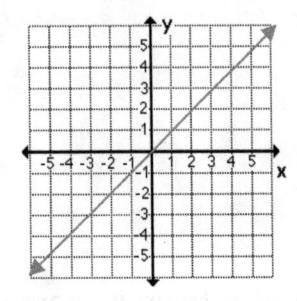

D.

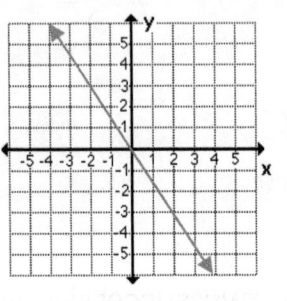

5) In the rectangle below if $y > 5$ cm and the area of rectangle is 50 cm^2 and the perimeter of the rectangle is 30 cm, what is the value of x and y respectively?

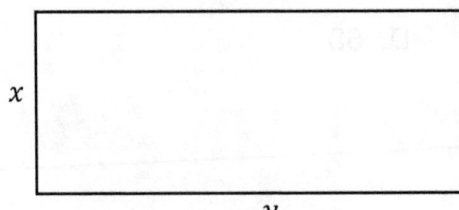

A. 4, 11
B. 5, 11
C. 5, 10
D. 4, 10

6) A football team had $40,000 to spend on supplies. The team spent $22,000 on new balls. New sport shoes cost $240 each. Which of the following inequalities represent how many new shoes the team can purchase.

A. $240x + 22,000 \leq 40,000$

B. $240x + 22,000 \geq 40,000$

C. $22,000x + 240 \leq 40,000$

D. $22,000x + 240 \geq 40,000$

7) Right triangle ABC has two legs of lengths 6 cm (AB) and 8 cm (AC). What is the length of the third side (BC)?

   A. 4 cm

   B. 6 cm

   C. 8 cm

   D. 10 cm

8) If $3x - 5 = 8.5$, What is the value of $5x + 3$?

   A. 13

   B. 15.5

   C. 20.5

   D. 25.5

9) A bank is offering 4.5% simple interest on a savings account. If you deposit $8,000, how much interest will you earn in five years?

   A. $360

   B. $720

   C. $1800

   D. $3600

10) In a party, 10 soft drinks are required for every 12 guests. If there are 252 guests, how many soft drink is required?

A. 21

B. 105

C. 210

D. 2510

This is the end of Session 1

Scientific Calculators are permitted for Session 2.

Time for Session 2: 60 Minutes

Session 2

11) A chemical solution contains 4% alcohol. If there is 24 ml of alcohol, what is the volume of the solution?

   A. 240 ml

   B. 480 ml

   C. 600 ml

   D. 1200 ml

12) What is the area of the shaded region?

   A. 31

   B. 40

   C. 64

   D. 80

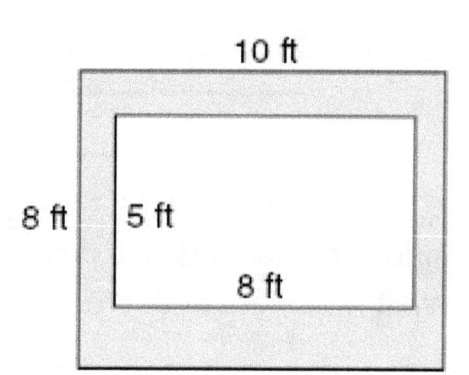

FSA Mathematics Workbook For Grade 8

13) A $40 shirt now selling for $28 is discounted by what percent?

   A. 20 %
   B. 30 %
   C. 40 %
   D. 60 %

14) How much interest is earned on a principal of $5000 invested at an interest rate of 5% for four years?

   A. $250
   B. $500
   C. $1000
   D. $2000

15) A swimming pool holds 2,000 cubic feet of water. The swimming pool is 25 feet long and 10 feet wide. How deep is the swimming pool?

   Write your answer in the box below.

   ☐

16) The price of a car was $20,000 in 2014, $16,000 in 2015 and $12,800 in 2016. What is the rate of depreciation of the price of car per year?

   A. 15 %
   B. 20 %
   C. 25 %
   D. 30 %

17) What is the area of the shaded region if the diameter of the bigger circle is 12 inches and the diameter of the smaller circle is 8 inches.

A. 16 π

B. 20 π

C. 36 π

D. 80 π

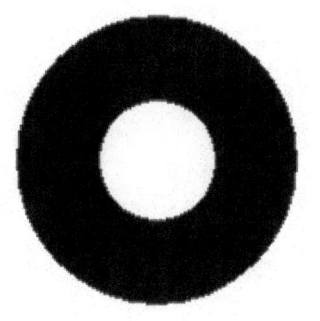

18) What is the area of an isosceles right triangle that has one leg that measures 6 cm?

Write your answer in the box below.

19) A taxi driver earns $9 per 1-hour work. If he works 10 hours a day and in 1 hour he uses 2-liters petrol with price $1 for 1-liter. How much money does he earn in one day?

A. $90

B. $88

C. $70

D. $60

20) Five years ago, Amy was three times as old as Mike was. If Mike is 10 years old now, how old is Amy?

A. 4
B. 8
C. 12
D. 20

This is the end of Session 2

Scientific Calculators are permitted for Session 3.

Time for Session 3: 60 Minutes

Session 3

21) What is the solution of the following system of equations?
$$\begin{cases} \dfrac{-x}{2} + \dfrac{y}{4} = 1 \\ \dfrac{-5y}{6} + 2x = 4 \end{cases}$$

A. $x = 48, y = 22$

B. $x = 50, y = 20$

C. $x = 20, y = 50$

D. $x = 22, y = 48$

22) What is the length of AB in the following figure if AE = 4, CD = 6 and AC = 12?

A. 3.8

B. 4.8

C. 7.2

D. 24

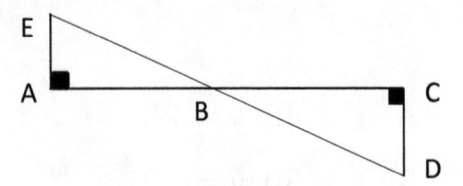

23) If a gas tank can hold 25 gallons, how many gallons does it contain when it is $\frac{2}{5}$ full?

A. 50

B. 125

C. 62.5

D. 10

24) In the xy-plane, the point $(4,3)$ and $(3,2)$ are on line A. Which of the following equations of lines is parallel to line A?

A. $y = 3x$

B. $y = \frac{x}{2}$

C. $y = 2x$

D. $y = x$

25) If x is directly proportional to the square of y, and $y = 2$ when $x = 12$, then when $x = 75$ $y = ?$

A. $\frac{1}{5}$

B. 1

C. 5

D. 12

26) Jack earns $616 for his first 44 hours of work in a week and is then paid 1.5 times his regular hourly rate for any additional hours. This week, Jack needs $826 to pay his rent, bills and other expenses. How many hours must he work to make enough money in this week?

A. 40

B. 48

C. 53

D. 54

Questions 27, 28 and 29 are based on the following data

Types of air pollutions in 10 cities of a country

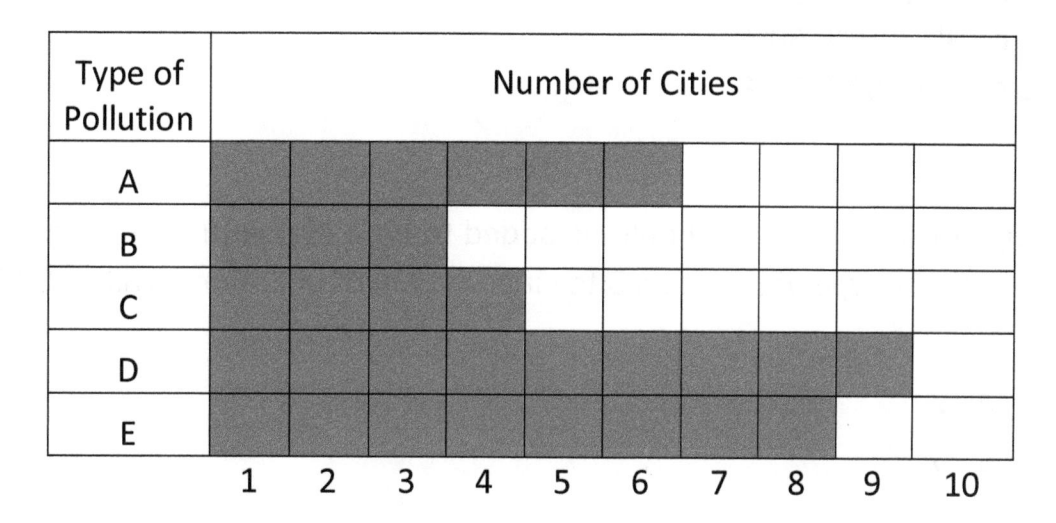

Type of Pollution	Number of Cities
A	6
B	3
C	4
D	9
E	8

27) If a is the mean (average) of the number of cities in each pollution type category, b is the mode, and c is the median of the number of cities in each pollution type category, then which of the following must be true?

A. $a < b < c$
B. $b < a < c$
C. $a = c$
D. $b < c = a$

28) What percent of cities are in the type of pollution A, C, and E respectively?

   A. 60%, 40%, 90%
   B. 30%, 40%, 90%
   C. 30%, 40%, 60%
   D. 40%, 60%, 90%

29) How many cities should be added to type of pollutions B until the ratio of cities in type of pollution B to cities in type of pollution E will be 0.625?

   A. 2

   B. 3

   C. 4

   D. 5

30) In the following right triangle, if the sides AB and AC become twice longer, what will be the ratio of the perimeter of the triangle to its area?

   A. $\frac{1}{2}$

   B. 2

   C. $\frac{1}{3}$

   D. 3

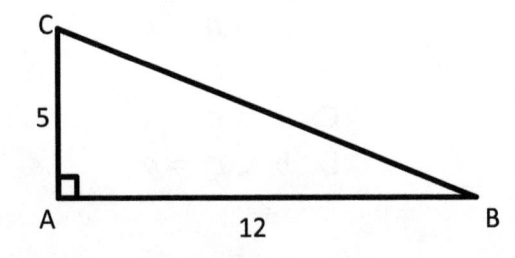

This is the end of Session 3

This is the end of Practice Test 1

FSA Mathematics Practice Test 2

The Florida Standards Assessments

Grade 8

Mathematics

2019

Scientific Calculators are NOT permitted for Session 1.

Time for Session 1: 60 Minutes

Session 1

FSA Mathematics Reference Sheet

Customary Conversions

1 foot = 12 inches

1 yard = 3 feet

1 mile = 5,280 feet

1 mile = 1,760 yards

1 cup = 8 fluid ounces

1 pint = 2 cups

1 quart = 2 pints

1 gallon = 4 quarts

1 pound = 16 ounces

1 ton = 2,000 pounds

Metric Conversions

1 meter = 100 centimeters

1 meter = 1000 millimeters

1 kilometer = 1000 meters

1 liter = 1000 milliliters

1 gram = 1000 milligrams

1 kilogram = 1000 grams

Time Conversions

1 minute = 60 seconds

1 hour = 60 minutes

1 day = 24 hours

1 year = 365 days

1 year = 52 weeks

Formulas

Area of parallelogram = base × height

Area of Rectangle = Length × Width

Volume = base × height

Volume of pyramid = $\frac{1}{3}$ *Bh*

Scientific Calculators are NOT permitted for Session 1.

Time for Session 1: 60 Minutes

Session 1

1) You can buy 5 cans of green beans at a supermarket for $3.40. How much does it cost to buy 35 cans of green beans?

   A. $17

   B. $23.80

   C. $34.00

   D. $119

2) Which of the following is the solution of the following inequality?

$$2x + 4 > 11x - 12.5 - 3.5x$$

   A. $x < 3$

   B. $x > 3$

   C. $x \leq 4$

   D. $x \geq 4$

3) What is the perimeter of a square that has an area of 595.36 feet?

   Write your answer in the box below.

4) A tree 32 feet tall casts a shadow 12 feet long. Jack is 6 feet tall. How long is Jack's shadow?

   A. 2.25 ft

   B. 4 ft

   C. 4.25 ft

   D. 8 ft

5) The price of a laptop is decreased by 10% to $360. What is its original price?

   A. 320

   B. 380

   C. 400

   D. 450

6) The perimeter of the trapezoid below is 54 cm. What is its area?

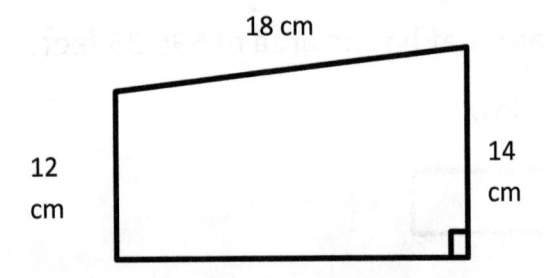

18 cm

12 cm

14 cm

Write your answer in the box below.

FSA Mathematics Workbook For Grade 8

7) Which graph does not represent y as a function of x?

A.

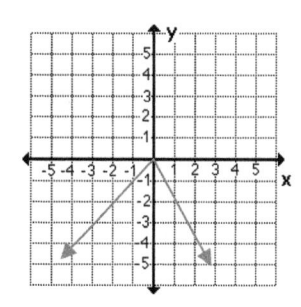

B.

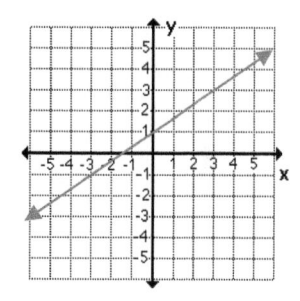

C.

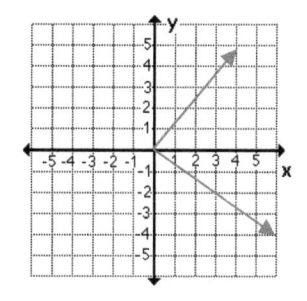

D.

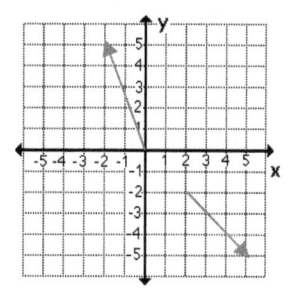

8) Which of the following is equivalent to $13 < -3x - 2 < 22$?

A. $-8 < x < -5$

B. $5 < x < 8$

C. $\frac{11}{3} < x < \frac{20}{3}$

D. $\frac{-20}{3} < x < \frac{-11}{3}$

www.EffortlessMath.com

9) In a certain bookshelf of a library, there are 35 biology books, 95 history books, and 80 language books. What is the ratio of the number of biology books to the total number of books in this bookshelf?

A. $\frac{1}{4}$

B. $\frac{1}{6}$

C. $\frac{2}{7}$

D. $\frac{3}{8}$

10) A bank is offering 3.5% simple interest on a savings account. If you deposit $12,000, how much interest will you earn in two years?

A. $420

B. $840

C. $4200

D. $8400

This is the end of Session 1

Scientific Calculators are permitted for Session 2.

Time for Session 2: 60 Minutes

Session 2

11) The area of a circle is 64 π. What is the circumference of the circle?

   E. 8 π
   F. 16 π
   G. 32 π
   H. 64 π

12) A shirt costing $200 is discounted 15%. After a month, the shirt is discounted another 15%. Which of the following expressions can be used to find the selling price of the shirt?

   A. (200) (0.70)
   B. (200) − 200 (0.30)
   C. (200) (0.15) − (200) (0.15)
   D. (200) (0.85) (0.85)

13) Joe scored 20 out of 25 marks in Algebra, 30 out of 40 marks in science and 68 out of 80 marks in mathematics. In which subject his percentage of marks is best?

   A. Algebra
   B. Science
   C. Mathematics
   D. Algebra and Science

14) What is the volume of the following triangular prism?

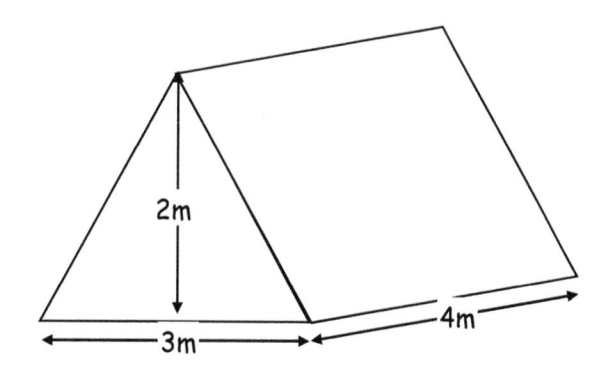

Write your answer in the box below.

15) The marked price of a computer is D dollar. Its price decreased by 20% in January and later increased by 10 % in February. What is the final price of the computer in D dollar?

A. 0.80 D
B. 0.88 D
C. 0.90 D
D. 1.20 D

16) Triangle ABC is graphed on a coordinate grid with vertices at A (−3, −2), B (−1, 4) and C (7, 9). Triangle ABC is reflected over x axes to create triangle A' B' C'.

Which order pair represents the coordinate of C'?

A. (7, 9)

B. (−7, −9)

C. (−7, 9)

D. (7, −9)

Questions 17 and 18 are based on the following data

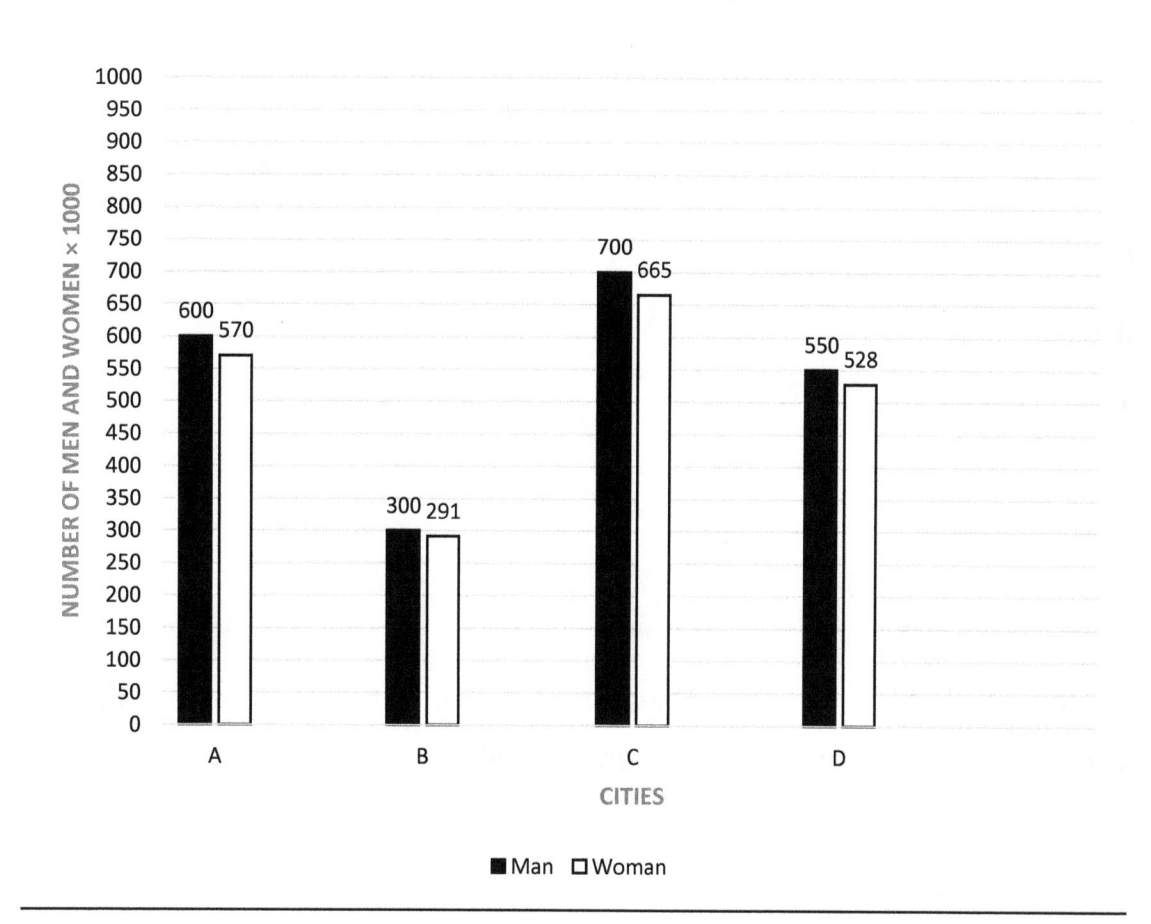

[Bar chart showing Number of Men and Women × 1000 for Cities A, B, C, D:
- A: Man 600, Woman 570
- B: Man 300, Woman 291
- C: Man 700, Woman 665
- D: Man 550, Woman 528]

17) What's the maximum ratio of woman to man in the four cities?

A. 0.98

B. 0.97

C. 0.96

D. 0.95

18) What's the ratio of percentage of men in city A to percentage of women in city C?

A. 0.9

B. 0.95

C. 1

D. 1.05

19) A container holds 3.5 gallons of water when it is $\frac{7}{24}$ full. How many gallons of water does the container hold when it's full?

A. 8

B. 12

C. 16

D. 20

20) If $(3^a)^b = 81$, then what is the value of $a \times b$?

A. 2

B. 3

C. 4

D. 5

This is the end of Session 2

Scientific Calculators are permitted for Session 3.

Time for Session 3: 60 Minutes

Session 3

21) Which of the following is equivalent to $13 < -3x - 2 < 22$?

A. $-8 < x < -5$

B. $5 < x < 8$

C. $\frac{11}{3} < x < \frac{20}{3}$

D. $\frac{-20}{3} < x < \frac{-11}{3}$

22) What is the x-intercept of the line with equation $2x - 2y = 5$?

A. -5

B. -2

C. $\frac{5}{2}$

D. $\frac{5}{4}$

23) Which of the following expressions is equivalent to $10 - \frac{2}{3}x \geq 12$

A. $x \geq -3$

B. $x \leq -3$

C. $x \geq 24\frac{1}{3}$

D. $x \leq 24\frac{1}{3}$

24) A soccer team played 120 games and won 70 percent of them. How many games did the team win?

   A. 84

   B. 94

   C. 104

   D. 114

25) Line m passes through the point (−1, 2). Which of the following CANNOT be the equation of line m?

   A. $y = 1 - x$

   B. $y = x + 1$

   C. $x = -1$

   D. $y = x + 3$

26) The equation of a line is given as: $y = 5x - 3$. Which of the following points does not lie on the line?

   A. (1, 2)

   B. (−2, −13)

   C. (3, 18)

   D. (2, 7)

27) The sum of three numbers is 45. If another number is added to these three numbers, the average of the four numbers is 20.

What is the fourth number?

A. 20

B. 35

C. 40

D. 45

28) David owed $8240. After making 45 payments of $124 each, how much did he have left to pay?

A. $2660

B. $3660

C. $5580

D. $6800

29) Find the slope–intercept form of the graph $6x - 7y = -12$

A. $y = -\frac{7}{6}x - \frac{12}{7}$

B. $y = -\frac{6}{7}x + 12$

C. $y = \frac{6}{7}x + \frac{12}{7}$

D. $y = \frac{7}{6}x - 12$

30) Which of the following point is the solution of the system of equations?

$$\begin{cases} 5x + y = 9 \\ 10x - 7y = -18 \end{cases}$$

A. (2, 4)

B. (2, 2)

C. (1, 4)

D. (0, 4)

This is the end of Session 3

This is the end of Practice Test 2

FSA Practice Tests
Answers and Explanations

FSA Math Practice Test 1				FSA Math Practice Test 2			
1	C	21	D	1	B	21	A
2	600	22	B	2	A	22	C
3	C	23	D	3	97.6	23	B
4	B	24	D	4	A	24	A
5	C	25	C	5	C	25	B
6	A	26	D	6	130	26	C
7	D	27	C	7	C	27	B
8	D	28	A	8	A	28	A
9	C	29	A	9	B	29	C
10	C	30	A	10	B	30	C
11	C			11	B		
12	B			12	D		
13	B			13	C		
14	C			14	12		
15	8			15	B		
16	B			16	D		
17	B			17	B		
18	18			18	D		
19	C			19	B		
20	D			20	C		

FSA Practice Test 1 Explanations

1) Choice C is correct

The weight of 12.2 meters of this rope is: 12.2 × 600 g = 7320 g

1kg = 1000 g, therefore, 7320 g ÷ 1000 = 7.32 kg

2) The correct answer is 600.

The ratio of boys to girls is 3:7. Therefore, there are 3 boys out of 10 students. To find the answer, first divide the number of boys by 3, then multiply the result by 10.

180 ÷ 3 = 60 ⇒ 60 × 10 = 600

3) Choice C is correct.

the population is increased by 15% and 20%. 15% increase changes the population to 115% of original population.

For the second increase, multiply the result by 120%.

(1.15) × (1.20) = 1.38 = 138%

38 percent of the population is increased after two years.

4) Choice B is correct.

A linear equation is a relationship between two variables, x and y, that can be put in the form $y = mx + b$.

A non-proportional linear relationship takes on the form $y = mx + b$, where $b \neq 0$ and its graph is a line that does not cross through the origin.

5) Choice C is correct

The perimeter of the rectangle is: $2x + 2y = 30 \rightarrow x + y = 15 \rightarrow x = 15 - y$

The area of the rectangle is: $x \times y = 50 \rightarrow (15 - y)(y) = 50 \rightarrow y^2 - 15y + 50 = 0$

Solve the quadratic equation by factoring method.

$(y - 5)(y - 10) = 0 \rightarrow y = 5$ (Unacceptable, because y must be greater than 5) or $y = 10$

If $y = 10 \rightarrow x \times y = 50 \rightarrow x \times 10 = 50 \rightarrow x = 5$

6) Choice A is correct.

Let x be the number of new shoes the team can purchase. Therefore, the team can purchase $240\,x$.

The team had $40,000 and spent $22,000. Now the team can spend on new shoes $18,000 at most.

Now, write the inequality: $120x + 22.000 \leq 40.000$

7) Choice D is correct

Use Pythagorean Theorem: $a^2 + b^2 = c^2$

$6^2 + 8^2 = c^2 \Rightarrow 100 = c^2 \Rightarrow c = 10$

8) Choice D is correct

$3x - 5 = 8.5 \rightarrow 3x = 8.5 + 5 = 13.5 \rightarrow x = \frac{13.5}{3} = 4.5$

Then; $5x + 3 = 5(4.5) + 3 = 22.5 + 3 = 25.5$

9) Choice C is correct

Use simple interest formula:

$I = prt$

(I = interest, p = principal, r = rate, t = time)

$$I = (8000)(0.045)(5) = 1800$$

10) Choice C is correct.

Let x be the number of soft drinks for 252 guests. Write the proportion and solve for x.

$\frac{10 \text{ soft drinks}}{12 \text{ guests}} = \frac{x}{252 \text{ guests}}$

$x = \frac{252 \times 10}{12} \Rightarrow x = 210$

11) Choice C is correct

4% of the volume of the solution is alcohol. Let x be the volume of the solution.

Then: 4% of x = 24 ml $\Rightarrow$ 0.04 x = 24 $\Rightarrow$ x = 24 ÷ 0.04 = 600

12) Choice B is correct

Use the area of rectangle formula (s = a × b).

To find area of the shaded region subtract smaller rectangle from bigger rectangle.

$S_1 - S_2$ = (10 ft × 8ft) − (5ft × 8ft) $\Rightarrow$ $S_1 - S_2$ = 40ft

13) Choice B is correct

Use the formula for Percent of Change

$$\frac{\text{New Value} - \text{Old Value}}{\text{Old Value}} \times 100\%$$

$\frac{28-40}{40} \times 100\% = -30\%$ (negative sign here means that the new price is less than old price).

14) Choice C is correct.

Use simple interest formula:

$I = prt$

(I = interest, p = principal, r = rate, t = time)

$$I = (5000)(0.05)(4) = 1000$$

15) The answer is 8.

Use formula of rectangle prism volume.

V = (length) (width) (height) ⇒ 2000 = (25) (10) (height) ⇒

height = 2000 ÷ 250 = 8

16) Choice B is correct.

Use this formula: Percent of Change

$$\frac{\text{New Value} - \text{Old Value}}{\text{Old Value}} \times 100\%$$

$\frac{16000-20000}{20000} \times 100\% = 20\%$ and $\frac{12800-16000}{16000} \times 100\% = 20\%$

17) Choice B is correct.

To find the area of the shaded region subtract smaller circle from bigger circle.

$S_{bigger} - S_{smaller} = \pi (r_{bigger})^2 - \pi (r_{smaller})^2 \Rightarrow S_{bigger} - S_{smaller} = \pi (6)^2 - \pi (4)^2$

$\Rightarrow 36\pi - 16\pi = 20\pi$

18) The answer is 18.

$a = 6 \Rightarrow$ area of the triangle is $= \frac{1}{2}(6 \times 6) = \frac{36}{2} = 18 \; cm^2$

Isosceles right triangle

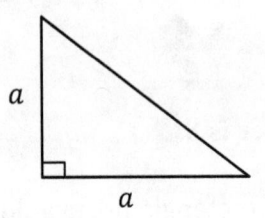

19) Choice C is correct

$\$9 \times 10 = \$90$

Petrol use: $10 \times 2 = 20$ liters

Petrol cost: $20 \times \$1 = \$20$

Money earned: $\$90 - \$20 = \$70$

20) Choice D is correct

Five years ago, Amy was three times as old as Mike. Mike is 10 years now. Therefore, 5 years ago Mike was 5 years.

Five years ago, Amy was: $A = 3 \times 5 = 15$

Now Amy is 20 years old: $15 + 5 = 20$

21) Choice D is correct

$\begin{cases} \frac{-x}{2} + \frac{y}{4} = 1 \\ \frac{-5y}{6} + 2x = 4 \end{cases} \rightarrow$ Multiply the top equation by 4. Then,

$\begin{cases} -2x + y = 4 \\ \frac{-5y}{6} + 2x = 4 \end{cases} \rightarrow$ Add two equations.

$\frac{1}{6} y = 8 \rightarrow y = 48$, plug in the value of y into the first equation $\rightarrow x = 22$

22) Choice B is correct

Two triangles ΔBAE and ΔBCD are similar. Then:

$$\frac{AE}{CD} = \frac{AB}{BC} \rightarrow \frac{4}{6} = \frac{x}{12} \rightarrow 48 - 4x = 6x \rightarrow 10x = 48 \rightarrow x = 4.8$$

23) Choice D is correct

$\frac{2}{5} \times 25 = \frac{50}{5} = 10$

24) Choice D is correct

The slop of line A is: $m = \frac{y_2 - y_1}{x_2 - x_1} = \frac{3-2}{4-3} = 1$

Parallel lines have the same slope and only choice D $(y = x)$ has slope of 1.

25) Choice C is correct

x is directly proportional to the square of y. Then:

$x = cy^2$

$$12 = c(2)^2 \rightarrow 12 = 4c \rightarrow c = \frac{12}{4} = 3$$

The relationship between x and y is:

$$x = 3y^2$$

$$x = 75$$

$$75 = 3y^2 \rightarrow y^2 = \frac{75}{3} = 25 \rightarrow y = 5$$

26) Choice D is correct

The amount of money that jack earns for one hour: $\frac{\$616}{44} = \$14$

Number of additional hours that he work to make enough money is: $\frac{\$826 - \$616}{1.5 \times \$14} = 10$

Number of total hours is: $44 + 10 = 54$

27) Choice C is correct

Let's find the mean (average), mode and median of the number of cities for each type of pollution.

Number of cities for each type of pollution: 6, 3, 4, 9, 8

$$average\ (mean) = \frac{sum\ of\ terms}{number\ of\ terms} = \frac{6+3+4+9+8}{5} = \frac{30}{5} = 6$$

Median is the number in the middle. To find median, first list numbers in order from smallest to largest.

3, 4, 6, 8, 9

Median of the data is 6.

Mode is the number which appears most often in a set of numbers. Therefore, there is no mode in the set of numbers.

Median = Mean, then, $a=c$

28) Choice A is correct

Percent of cities in the type of pollution A: $\frac{6}{10} \times 100 = 60\%$

Percent of cities in the type of pollution C: $\frac{4}{10} \times 100 = 40\%$

Percent of cities in the type of pollution E: $\frac{9}{10} \times 100 = 90\%$

29) Choice A is correct

Let the number of cities should be added to type of pollutions B be x. Then:

$\frac{x+3}{8} = 0.625 \rightarrow x + 3 = 8 \times 0.625 \rightarrow x + 3 = 5 \rightarrow x = 2$

30) Choice A is correct

$AB = 12$ And $AC = 5$

$BC = \sqrt{12^2 + 5^2} = \sqrt{144 + 25} = \sqrt{169} = 13$

Perimeter $= 5 + 12 + 13 = 30$

Area $= \frac{5 \times 12}{2} = 5 \times 6 = 30$

In this case, the ratio of the perimeter of the triangle to its area is: $\frac{30}{30} = 1$

If the sides AB and AC become twice longer, then:

$AB = 24$ And $AC = 10$

$BC = \sqrt{24^2 + 10^2} = \sqrt{576 + 100} = \sqrt{676} = 26$

Perimeter $= 26 + 24 + 10 = 60$

Area $= \frac{10 \times 24}{2} = 10 \times 12 = 120$

In this case the ratio of the perimeter of the triangle to its area is: $\frac{60}{120} = \frac{1}{2}$

FSA Practice Test 2 Explanations

1) **Choice B is correct**

Let x be the number of cans. Write the proportion and solve for x.

$\frac{5 \text{ cans}}{\$\,3.40} = \frac{35 \text{ cans}}{x}$

$x = \frac{3.40 \times 35}{5} \Rightarrow x = \$23.8$

2) **Choice A is correct**

$2x + 4 > 11x - 12.5 - 3.5x \rightarrow$ Combine like terms:

$2x + 4 > 7.5x - 12.5 \rightarrow$ Subtract $2x$ from both sides: $4 > 5.5x - 12.5$

Add 12.5 both sides of the inequality.

$16.5 > 5.5x$, Divide both sides by 5.5.

$\frac{16.5}{5.5} > x \rightarrow x < 3$

3) **The correct answer is 97.6 feet.**

Area of a square: $S = a^2 \Rightarrow 595.36 = a^2 \Rightarrow a = 24.4$

Perimeter of a square: $P = 4a \Rightarrow P = 4 \times 24.4 \Rightarrow P = 97.6$

4) Choice A is correct.

Write the proportion and solve for the missing number.

$\frac{32}{12} = \frac{6}{x} \rightarrow 32x = 6 \times 12 = 72$

$$32x = 72 \rightarrow x = \frac{72}{32} = 2.25$$

5) Choice C is correct.

Let x be the original price.

If the price of a laptop is decreased by 10% to $360, then:

$90\ \% \ of\ x = 360 \Rightarrow 0.90x = 360 \Rightarrow x = 360 \div 0.90 = 400$

6) The answer is 130.

The perimeter of the trapezoid is 54 cm.

Therefore, the missing side (high) is = 54 − 18 − 12 − 14 = 10

Area of a trapezoid: A = $\frac{1}{2}$ h (b_1 + b_2) = $\frac{1}{2}$ (10) (12 + 14) = 130

7) Choice C is correct.

A graph represents y as a function of x if

$x_1 = x_2 \rightarrow y_1 = y_2$

In choice C, for each x, we have two different values for y.

8) Choice A is correct

$13 < -3x - 2 < 22 \to$ Add 2 to all sides.

$13 + 2 < -3x - 2 + 2 < 22 + 2$

$\to 15 < -3x < 24 \to$ Divide all sides by -3. (Remember that when you divide all sides of an inequality by a negative number, the inequality sing will be swapped. < becomes >)

$$\frac{15}{-3} > \frac{-3x}{-3} > \frac{24}{-3}$$

$-8 < x < -5$

9) Choice B is correct

Number of biology book: 35

Total number of books; $35 + 95 + 80 = 210$

The ratio of the number of biology books to the total number of books is: $\frac{35}{210} = \frac{1}{6}$

10) Choice B is correct

Use simple interest formula:

$I = prt$

(I = interest, p = principal, r = rate, t = time)

$$I = (12000)(0.035)(2) = 840$$

11) Choice B is correct

Use the formula for area of circles.

Area = $\pi r^2 \Rightarrow 64\pi = \pi r^2 \Rightarrow 64 = r^2 \Rightarrow r = 8$

Radius of the circle is 8. Now, use the circumference formula:

Circumference = $2\pi r = 2\pi(8) = 16\pi$

12) Choice D is correct

To find the discount, multiply the number by (100% − rate of discount).

Therefore, for the first discount we get: (200) (100% − 15%) = (200) (0.85)

For the next 15 % discount: (200) (0.85) (0.85)

13) Choice C is correct.

Compare each mark:

In Algebra Joe scored 20 out of 25 in Algebra. It means Joe scored 80% of the total mark.

$\frac{20}{25} = \frac{x}{100} \Rightarrow x = 80\%$

Joe scored 30 out of 40 in science. It means Joe scored 75% of the total mark.

$\frac{30}{40} = \frac{x}{100} \Rightarrow x = 75\%$

Joe scored 68 out of 80 in mathematic that it means 85% of total mark.

$\frac{68}{80} = \frac{x}{100} \Rightarrow x = 85\%$

Therefore, his score in mathematic is higher than his other scores.

14) The correct answer is 12m³.

Use the volume of the triangular prism formula.

$V = \frac{1}{2}$ (length) (base) (high)

$V = \frac{1}{2} \times 4 \times 3 \times 2 \Rightarrow V = 12 \text{ m}^3$

15) Choice B is correct

To find the discount, multiply the price by (100% − rate of discount).

Therefore, for the first discount we get: (D) (100% − 20%) = (D) (0.80) = 0.80 D

To increase the 10 %: (0.80 D) (100% + 10%) = (0.85 D) (1.10) = 0.88 D = 88% of D

16) Choice D is correct.

When a point is reflected over x axes, the (y) coordinate of that point changes to ($-y$) while its x coordinate remains the same.

C (7, 9) → C' (7, −9)

17) Choice B is correct

Ratio of women to men in city A: $\frac{570}{600} = 0.95$

Ratio of women to men in city B: $\frac{291}{300} = 0.97$

Ratio of women to men in city C: $\frac{665}{700} = 0.95$

Ratio of women to men in city D: $\frac{528}{550} = 0.96$

18) Choice D is correct

Percentage of men in city A = $\frac{600}{1170} \times 100 = 51.28\%$

Percentage of women in city C = $\frac{665}{1365} \times 100 = 48.72\%$

Percentage of men in city A to percentage of women in city C = $\frac{51.28}{48.72} = 1.05$

19) Choice B is correct

let x be the number of gallons of water the container holds when it is full.

Then; $\frac{7}{24}x = 3.5 \rightarrow x = \frac{24 \times 3.5}{7} = 12$

20) Choice C is correct

$(3^a)^b = 81 \rightarrow 3^{ab} = 81$

$81 = 3^4 \rightarrow 3^{ab} = 3^4$

$\rightarrow ab = 4$

21) Choice A is correct

$13 < -3x - 2 < 22 \rightarrow$ Add 2 to all sides.

$13 + 2 < -3x - 2 + 2 < 22 + 2$

$\rightarrow 15 < -3x < 24 \rightarrow$ Divide all sides by -3. (Remember that when you divide all sides of an inequality by a negative number, the inequality sing will be swapped. < becomes >)

$\frac{15}{-3} > \frac{-3x}{-3} > \frac{24}{-3}$

$-8 < x < -5$

22) Choice C is correct

The value of y in the x-intercept of a line is zero. Then:

300

$y = 0 \to 2x - 2(0) = 5 \to 2x = 5 \to x = \dfrac{5}{2}$

then, x-intercept of the line is $\dfrac{5}{2}$

23) Choice B is correct

Simplify:

$10 - \dfrac{2}{3}x \geq 12 \Rightarrow -\dfrac{2}{3}x \geq 2 \Rightarrow -x \geq 3 \Rightarrow x \leq -3$

24) Choice A is correct

$120 \times \dfrac{70}{100} = 84$

25) Choice B is correct

Solve for each equation:

(−1, 2)

$y = 1 - x \Rightarrow 2 = 1 - (-1) \Rightarrow 2 = 2$

$y = x + 1 \Rightarrow 2 = -1 + 1 \Rightarrow 2 \neq 0$

$x = -1 \Rightarrow -1 = -1$

$y = x + 3 \Rightarrow 2 = -1 + 3 \Rightarrow 2 = 2$

26) Choice C is correct

$y = 5x - 3$

(1, 2) $\Rightarrow 2 = 5 - 3$ $\Rightarrow 2 = 2$

(−2, −13) $\Rightarrow -13 = -10 - 3$ $\Rightarrow -13 = -13$

(3, 18) $\Rightarrow 18 = 15 - 3$ $\Rightarrow 18 \neq 12$

(2, 7) $\Rightarrow 7 = 10 - 3$ $\Rightarrow 7 = 7$

27) Choice B is correct

$a + b + c = 45$

$\dfrac{a+b+c+d}{4} = 20$ $\Rightarrow$ $a + b + c + d = 80$ $\Rightarrow 45 + d = 80$

$d = 80 - 45 = 35$

28) Choice A is correct

$45 \times \$124 = \$5580$ Payable amount is: $\$8240 - \$5580 = \$2660$

29) Choice C is correct

$-7y = -6x - 12 \Rightarrow y = \dfrac{-6}{-7}x - \dfrac{12}{-7} \Rightarrow y = \dfrac{6}{7}x + \dfrac{12}{7}$

30) Choice C is correct

$\begin{cases} 5x + y = 9 \\ 10x - 7y = -18 \end{cases}$ $\Rightarrow$ Multiply (-2) to the first equation $\Rightarrow \begin{cases} -10x - 2y = -18 \\ 10x - 7y = -18 \end{cases}$

Add two equations together $\Rightarrow -9y = -36 \Rightarrow y = 4$, then: $x = 1$

"Effortless Math Education" Publications

Effortless Math Education authors' team strives to prepare and publish the best quality Mathematics learning resources to make learning Math easier for all. We hope that our publications help you or your student learn Math in an effective way.

We all in Effortless Math wish you good luck and successful studies!

Effortless Math Authors

Online Math Lessons

Enjoy interactive Math lessons online

with the best Math teachers

Online Math learning that's effective, affordable, flexible, and fun

Learn Math wherever you want; when you want
Ultimate flexibility. You can now learn Math online, enjoy high quality engaging lessons no matter where in the world you are. It's affordable too.

Learn Math with one-on-one classes
We provide one-on-one Math tutoring online. We believe that one-to-one tutoring is the most effective way to learn Math.

Qualified Math tutors
Working with the best Math tutors in the world is the key to success! Our tutors give you the support and motivation you need to succeed with a personal touch.

Online Math Lessons

It's easy! Here's how it works.

1- Request a FREE introductory session.

2- Meet a Math tutor online.

3- Start Learning Math in Minutes.

Send Email to: info@EffortlessMath.com